Focus on GRAMMAR 4

FOURTH EDITION

Marjorie Fuchs
Margaret Bonner

with Jane Curtis

Zen Koo

ALWAYS LEARNING

PEARSON

FOCUS ON GRAMMAR 4: An Integrated Skills Approach, Fourth Edition
Workbook

Copyright © 2012, 2006, 2000, 1995 by Pearson Education, Inc.
All rights reserved.

Pearson Education, Inc., 10 Bank Street, White Plains, NY 10606

Staff credits: The people who made up the ***Focus on Grammar 4, Fourth Edition,***
  Workbook team, representing editorial, production, design, and manufacturing, are: Aerin Csigay,
  Christine Edmonds, Nancy Flaggman, Ann France, Stacey Hunter, Lise Minovitz, and Robert Ruvo.

Cover image: Shutterstock.com
Text composition: ElectraGraphics, Inc.
Text font: New Aster

Photo credits: **Page 6** PictureQuest; **p. 18** WENN Photos/Newscom; **p. 22** Derek Storm/Splash News/Newscom;
  p. 27 Jumanah EI Heloueh/Reuters/Corbis; **p. 44** Jane Curtis; **p. 56** Shutterstock.com; **p. 62** UPI/Landov;
  p. 67 Shutterstock.com; **p. 74** Shutterstock.com; **p. 106** Shutterstock.com; **p. 140** General Photographic
  Agency/Getty Images; **p. 143** Disney/Pixar/Photofest; **p. 169** Paul J. Richards/Getty Images

Illustrations: **ElectraGraphics, Inc.:** pp. 32, 50, 57, 93, 94, 104, 108, 116, 121, 123, 145, 163

ISBN 10: 0-13-216941-X
ISBN 13: 978-0-13-216941-7

Printed in the United States of America

3 4 5 6 7 8 9 10—V001—16 15 14 13

CONTENTS

ABOUT THE AUTHORS

Marjorie Fuchs has taught ESL at New York City Technical College and LaGuardia Community College of the City University of New York and EFL at the Sprach Studio Lingua Nova in Munich, Germany. She has a master's degree in Applied English Linguistics and a Certificate in TESOL from the University of Wisconsin–Madison. She has authored and co-authored many widely used books and multimedia materials, notably *Crossroads, Top Twenty ESL Word Games: Beginning Vocabulary Development, Families: Ten Card Games for Language Learners, Focus on Grammar 4: An Integrated Skills Approach, Focus on Grammar 3 CD-ROM, Focus on Grammar 4 CD-ROM, Longman English Interactive 3 and 4, Grammar Express Basic, Grammar Express Basic CD-ROM, Grammar Express Intermediate, Future 1: English for Results,* and workbooks for *The Oxford Picture Dictionary High Beginning* and *Low Intermediate,* and *Focus on Grammar 3* and *4.*

Margaret Bonner has taught ESL at Hunter College and the Borough of Manhattan Community College of the City University of New York, at Taiwan National University in Taipei, and at Virginia Commonwealth University in Richmond. She holds a master's degree in Library Science from Columbia University, and she has done work toward a Ph.D. in English Literature at the Graduate Center of the City University of New York. She has authored and co-authored numerous ESL and EFL print and multimedia materials, including textbooks for the national school system of Oman, *Step into Writing: A Basic Writing Text, Focus on Grammar 4: An Integrated Skills Approach, Focus on Grammar 4 Workbook, Grammar Express Basic, Grammar Express Basic CD-ROM, Grammar Express Basic Workbook, Grammar Express Intermediate, Focus on Grammar 3 CD-ROM, Focus on Grammar 4 CD-ROM, Longman English Interactive 4,* and *The Oxford Picture Dictionary Low-Intermediate Workbook.*

Jane Curtis began teaching ESOL in Spain, where she participated in a Fulbright exchange program between the University of Barcelona and the University of Illinois at Urbana–Champaign. She currently teaches at Roosevelt University in Chicago, Illinois. She holds a master's degree in Spanish from the University of Illinois at Urbana–Champaign and a master's degree in Applied Linguistics from Northeastern Illinois University.

PART I

PRESENT AND PAST:
REVIEW AND EXPANSION

UNIT 1 Simple Present and Present Progressive

EXERCISE 1: Spelling: Simple Present and Present Progressive

Write the correct forms of the verbs.

Base Form	Simple Present Third-Person Singular	Present Participle
1. answer	answers	answering
2. _____	asks	_____
3. buy	_____	_____
4. _____	_____	coming
5. _____	does	_____
6. eat	_____	_____
7. _____	_____	employing
8. _____	_____	flying
9. forget	_____	_____
10. _____	has	_____
11. hurry	_____	_____
12. _____	_____	lying
13. open	_____	_____
14. rain	_____	_____
15. reach	_____	_____
16. _____	says	_____
17. tie	_____	_____
18. _____	_____	controlling

EXERCISE 2: Simple Present and Present Progressive

Complete the conversations with the correct form of the verbs in parentheses—simple present or present progressive. Use contractions when possible.

A. AMBER: I _____*think*_____ I've seen you before. _____ you
1. (think)

_____ Professor Bertolucci's course this semester?
2. (take)

NOËL: No, but my twin sister, Dominique, _____ Italian this year.
3. (study)

AMBER: That _____ her! I _____ her name now. You two
4. (be)   5. (remember)

_____ exactly alike.
6. (look)

B. JARED: _____ you _____ that woman over there?
1. (know)

TARO: That's Mangena. She usually _____ a pronunciation class at the Institute,
2. (teach)

but she _____ in the computer lab this term.
3. (work)

JARED: That's an interesting name. What _____ it _____?
4. (mean)

TARO: I'm not sure. It's certainly not a name that's in style. I _____ I've ever
5. (not believe)

known anyone else with that name.

C. ROSA: How _____ you _____ your name?
1. (spell)

ZHUŌ: Here, I'll write it down for you.

ROSA: You _____ unusual handwriting. It _____ very artistic.
2. (have)   3. (look)

D. IVY: Hi. Why _____ you _____ there with such a terrible look
1. (sit)

on your face? You _____ too happy.
2. (not seem)

LEE: I _____ to read this letter from my friend. He _____ to
3. (try)   4. (not like)

use a computer, so he _____ his letters by hand and his handwriting
5. (write)

_____ awful. It _____ to get on my nerves.
6. (be)   7. (begin)

E. AMY: _____ you _____ to hear something interesting? Justin
1. (want)

_____ to become a graphologist.
2. (study)

CHRIS: What exactly _____ a graphologist _____?
3. (do)

AMY: A graphologist _____ people's handwriting. You can learn a lot
4. (analyze)

about people from the way they _____—especially from how they
5. (write)

_____ their name.
6. (sign)

EXERCISE 3: Simple Present and Present Progressive

Complete the article. Use the correct form of the verbs in parentheses—simple present or present progressive. Sometimes there is more than one correct answer.

Right now, Pam O'Neil _____is taking_____ a test, but she _____ it. She
             1. (take)   **2. (not know)**

_____ on what she _____, and not on how her handwriting
3. (focus)   **4. (write)**

_____. The person who will analyze that test is a graphologist—someone who
5. (look)

_____ handwriting. Graphologists _____ that a person's
6. (study)   **7. (believe)**

handwriting _____ an indication of his or her personality and character. These
8. (give)

days, a number of businesses _____ graphologists. Handwriting sometimes
9. (use)

_____ employers to hire one job applicant over another.
10. (convince)

What exactly _____ company graphologist Perry Vance _____
                                                             11. (hope)

to learn from applicants' writing samples? "I always _____ for clues to possible
                                           12. (look)

behavior," he explained. "For example, the slant of the writing actually _____ a
                                               13. (tell)

lot. _____ the writing _____ to the left or to the right? A left slant
                                  14. (lean)

often _____ a shy personality. The position of the sample on the page is also
       15. (indicate)

important," Vance continued. "The right-hand margin of the page _____ the
                                           16. (represent)

future. Here's a writing sample from an executive who right now _____ a new
                                             17. (plan)

direction for a large company. Notice that this person _____ much room in the
                                    18. (not leave)

right-hand margin. This is someone who _____ looking at the future."
                               19. (not avoid)

"What about signatures?" I asked. "Yes, signatures _____ us a lot about
                                      20. (show)

someone," said Vance, "Look at this one by a chief executive officer of a large firm. He

_____ on the news a lot these days because the federal government
21. (be)

_____ his company. Those very large strokes are typical of a person who
22. (investigate)

_____ about himself first and _____ advantage of other people."
23. (think)   **24. (take)**

Vance always _____, however, that his analysis _____ an
                 25. (warn)   **26. (not guarantee)**

applicant's future job performance. It's no substitute for careful review of a complete application.

EXERCISE 4: Editing

Read the email from a student to her favorite English teacher. There are ten mistakes in the use of the simple present and the present progressive. The first mistake is already corrected. Find and correct nine more.

Dear Professor,

    Well, I'm here at my new school, and ~~I'm liking~~ *I like* it very much. I'm study in the English Institute this semester, and the style of the classes is really different from our English classes in Korea. My teachers doesn't know how to speak Korean, and my classmates are coming from countries all around the world, so we use English all the time. That is meaning that I'm getting a lot of good practice these days.

    Although I'm very happy, sometimes I'm having problems. I'm not understand my classmates' names because they don't look or sound like Korean names. I always ask the same questions: "What's your name?" and "How you spell it?" I want to use names with titles like "Mr. Hoffman" and "Prof. Li" for my teachers, but they want me to call them by their first names. It's difficult for me to treat my teachers so informally, but I trying. Slowly but surely, I'm getting accustomed to my life here.

    I miss you a lot. You still my favorite English teacher.

Hye Lee

EXERCISE 5: Personal Writing

On a separate piece of paper, write a paragraph about popular names in your home country. Use some of the phrases from the box.

In general . . .	These days . . .
In my country, people always . . .	We don't usually . . .
More and more . . .	We never . . .
Now, in the 21st century . . .	We sometimes . . .

UNIT 2 Simple Past and Past Progressive

EXERCISE 1: Spelling: Regular and Irregular Simple Past Forms

Write the correct forms of the verbs.

Base Form	Simple Past
1. _____agree_____	agreed
2. _____	applied
3. be	_____ OR _____
4. become	_____
5. carry	_____
6. develop	_____
7. _____	ate
8. fall	_____
9. _____	felt
10. get	_____
11. grow	_____
12. live	_____
13. _____	met
14. _____	paid
15. permit	_____
16. plan	_____
17. _____	sent
18. sleep	_____

Complete the magazine article. Use the correct form of the verbs in parentheses—simple past or past progressive. Sometimes there is more than one correct answer.

First Meetings
by Rebecca Hubbard

$\mathcal{W}$hat _____were_____ you _____doing_____ when you first
                    1.(do)
_____ that special person in
         2.(meet)
your life? A few months ago, we

_____ some couples to answer
         3.(ask)
these questions. _____ it love at first sight, or _____ you
                          4.(be)
hardly _____ each other? _____ you _____
              5.(notice)   **6.(go)**
out with someone else before you _____ your One True Love? Read some
                                          7.(find)
of the great stories from our readers.

$\mathcal{D}$ana and I sure _____ in love at first sight! We _____
                          8.(not fall)   **9.(work)**
in the same consumer research office when we _____. At the time the
                                                      10.(meet)
company _____ me, she _____ to get a promotion. It
                11.(hire)   **12.(try)**
_____ my very first job. I _____ a little scared, so I
      13.(be)   **14.(feel)**
_____ to know everything. Of course Dana _____ I
      15.(pretend)   **16.(think)**
_____ to get the promotion instead of her. But then, one day I
      17.(want)
_____ on a problem when she _____ into my office. I
      18.(work)   **19.(come)**
_____ her for help at first, but I was stuck, so finally I did. And guess
      20.(not ask)
what! She _____ the problem! So then we _____ acting
              21.(solve)   **22.(stop)**
like opponents and treated each other like members of the same team. Eventually, we

_____ in love.
      23.(fall)

$\mathcal{V}$an has been influential in my life since we were teenagers. We _____
24. (take)
the same high school social studies class when we _____. We
25. (meet)
_____ friends right away. At the time, I _____ someone
26. (become) **27. (date)**
else, and Van _____ interested in a romantic relationship. One day, the
28. (not seem)
teacher _____ me while I _____ to Van. The teacher
29. (hear) **30. (whisper)**
_____ angry at us for talking during class, and she _____
31. (get) **32. (tell)**
both of us to stay after school. I _____ to complain about such a severe
33. (want)
punishment, but then I _____ my mind because I _____
34. (change) **35. (realize)**
that staying late after school with a good friend might be fun. That afternoon, Van and I
_____ talking. We covered everything from our favorite music to our
36. (not stop)
goals in life. As soon as I _____ with my old boyfriend, Van
37. (break up)
_____ me out.
38. (ask)

$\mathcal{A}$leesha _____ into the apartment next door to mine when I
39. (move)
__ _____ her for the first time. I _____ on the front steps
40. (see) **41. (sit)**
while she _____ to park a U-Haul moving truck in front of the apartment
42. (try)
building. As soon as she _____ out of the truck, I _____,
43. (jump) **44. (think)**
"I'm going to marry that woman." I _____ her out right away because a
45. (not ask)
guy _____ her move. He _____ like her boyfriend.
46. (help) **47. (seem)**
One day I _____ Aleesha and her "boyfriend" in the hall. She
48. (see)
_____ me to her brother! I _____ her to dinner the
49. (introduce) **50. (invite)**
next weekend.

EXERCISE 3: Simple Past and Past Progressive

*Use the cues to write sentences about Joao's first date with Dana. Use **when** or **while** and the simple past or past progressive form of each verb. There is more than one way to write some of the sentences.*

1. drops his wallet / waits for Dana in the restaurant

   He dropped his wallet while he was waiting for Dana in the restaurant.

2. drinks a glass of water / breaks the glass

   _____

3. stands up to greet Dana / falls on the wet floor

   _____

4. forgets Dana's name / wants to introduce her to a friend

   _____

5. eats a plate of spaghetti / gets some sauce on Dana's dress

   _____

6. has no money / gets the check at the end of dinner

   _____

7. thinks only about Dana / drives home

   _____

8. receives a phone call from Dana / recovers from his car accident

   _____

EXERCISE 2: Simple Present and Present Progressive

Complete the conversations with the correct form of the verbs in parentheses—simple present or present progressive. Use contractions when possible.

A. **AMBER:** I _____*think*_____ I've seen you before. _____ you
                 1. (think)

        _____ Professor Bertolucci's course this semester?
        2. (take)

    NOËL: No, but my twin sister, Dominique, _____ Italian this year.
                                            3. (study)

    AMBER: That _____ her! I _____ her name now. You two
                    4. (be)   **5. (remember)**

        _____ exactly alike.
        6. (look)

B. **JARED:** _____ you _____ that woman over there?
                             1. (know)

    TARO: That's Mangena. She usually _____ a pronunciation class at the Institute,
                                2. (teach)

        but she _____ in the computer lab this term.
                  3. (work)

    JARED: That's an interesting name. What _____ it _____?
                                            4. (mean)

    TARO: I'm not sure. It's certainly not a name that's in style. I _____ I've ever
                                              5. (not believe)

        known anyone else with that name.

C. **ROSA:** How _____ you _____ your name?
                             1. (spell)

    ZHUŌ: Here, I'll write it down for you.

    ROSA: You _____ unusual handwriting. It _____ very artistic.
                  2. (have)   **3. (look)**

D. **IVY:** Hi. Why _____ you _____ there with such a terrible look
                             1. (sit)

        on your face? You _____ too happy.
                   2. (not seem)

    LEE: I _____ to read this letter from my friend. He _____ to
             3. (try)   **4. (not like)**

        use a computer, so he _____ his letters by hand and his handwriting
                          5. (write)

        _____ awful. It _____ to get on my nerves.
        6. (be)   **7. (begin)**

E. **AMY:** _____ you _____ to hear something interesting? Justin
                             1. (want)

        _____ to become a graphologist.
        2. (study)

    CHRIS: What exactly _____ a graphologist _____?
                                          3. (do)

    AMY: A graphologist _____ people's handwriting. You can learn a lot
                            4. (analyze)

        about people from the way they _____—especially from how they
                                5. (write)

        _____ their name.
        6. (sign)

UNIT 1   Simple Present and Present Progressive

EXERCISE 1: Spelling: Simple Present and Present Progressive

Write the correct forms of the verbs.

Base Form	Simple Present Third-Person Singular	Present Participle
1. answer	answers	answering
2. _____	asks	_____
3. buy	_____	_____
4. _____	_____	coming
5. _____	does	_____
6. eat	_____	_____
7. _____	_____	employing
8. _____	_____	flying
9. forget	_____	_____
10. _____	has	_____
11. hurry	_____	_____
12. _____	_____	lying
13. open	_____	_____
14. rain	_____	_____
15. reach	_____	_____
16. _____	says	_____
17. tie	_____	_____
18. _____	_____	controlling

EXERCISE 4: Editing

Read the entry from Aleesha's journal. There are nine mistakes in the use of the simple past and the past progressive. The first mistake is already corrected. Find and correct eight more.

December 16

                              decided

    I'm really glad that I ~~was deciding~~ to rent this apartment. I almost wasn't move here because the rent is a little high, but I'm happy to be here. All the other apartments I researched were seeming too small, and the neighborhoods just weren't as beautiful as this one. And moving wasn't as bad as I feared. My original plan was to take a week off from work, but when Hakim was offering to help, I didn't need so much time. What a great brother! We were moving everything into the apartment in two days. The man next door was really nice to us. On the second day, he even helped Hakim with some of the heavy furniture. His name is Jared. I don't even unpack the kitchen stuff last weekend because I was so tired. Last night I walking Mitzi for only two blocks. When I came back, Jared stood downstairs. I think I made him nervous because he was dropping his mail when he saw me. When he recovered, we talked for a few minutes. I'd like to ask him over for coffee this weekend (in order to thank him), but everything is still in boxes. Maybe in a couple of weeks . . .

EXERCISE 5: Personal Writing

On a separate piece of paper, write a paragraph about your favorite married couple (your parents, an aunt and uncle, family friends, etc.). Tell a story that shows why you really like them. Use some of the phrases from the box.

After they . . .	I felt . . . after . . .
As soon as . . .	I remember the time when . . .
Before this experience . . .	Let me give some background information . . .
Here's what happened . . .	They . . . while . . .
I chose to write about . . . because . . .	When I . . .
I didn't . . . until . . .	

Simple Past, Present Perfect, and Present Perfect Progressive

EXERCISE 1: Spelling: Simple Past and Present Perfect

Write the correct forms of the verbs.

Base Form	Simple Past	Past Participle
1. become	*became*	*become*
2. bring		
3. choose		
4. delay		
5. feel		
6. find		
7. finish		
8. get		
9. graduate		
10. hide		
11. notice		
12. omit		
13. own		
14. read		
15. reply		
16. rip		
17. show		
18. speak		

A. *Look at the reporter's notes about the bride and groom.*

THE SKOAP–POHLIG WEDDING
BACKGROUND INFORMATION

Bride	Groom
Nakisha Skoap	Simon Pohlig
born in Broadfield	started doing extreme sports in 2004
lived here all her life	moved to Broadfield in 2006
B.A. Claremont College, 2005	bought Broadview's historic Sharney's
2002—Began working for	Restaurant in 2008; met Nakisha
Broadfield Examiner	Skoap at the restaurant
2008—became crime news reporter	basketball coach for Boys and Girls Club
and started master's degree	2007–2009
program in political science	proposed marriage to Nakisha last year
started research on crime in	author of Simon Says and Duck Soup,
schools in Jan.	kids' cookbooks
Father—James Skoap, joined the	in Jan. started developing local TV show
Broadfield Police Department in	Mother—Tina Pohlig, fantastic chef.
1989, retired in 2009	Seven years as president of TLC
	Meals, Inc., but plans to retire soon

(continued on next page)

B. *Write statements about the bride and groom, using the words in parentheses. Use the simple past, present perfect, or present perfect progressive form of the verbs. Add any necessary words to the time expressions.*

1. (Nakisha Skoap / live in Broadfield / all her life)

   Nakisha Skoap has lived in Broadfield all her life.

2. (she / graduate / from college / 2005)

   _____

3. (report / crime news / 2008)

   _____

4. (recently / research / crime in schools)

   _____

5. (work / on her master's degree / 2008)

   _____

6. (her father / work / for the Broadfield Police Department / 20 years)

   _____

7. (Simon Pohlig / move / to Broadfield / 2006)

   _____

8. (own / the historic Sharney's Restaurant / 2008)

   _____

9. (A friend / introduce / Simon and Nakisha / at the restaurant / one night)

   _____

10. (coach / basketball / for the Boys and Girls Club / two years)

    _____

11. (write / two cookbooks for children)

    _____

12. (plan / a local television show / January of this year)

    _____

13. (Nakisha and Simon / be engaged / one year)

    _____

A. *Look at Nakisha's job application. Then complete the personnel officer's notes on page 14.*

CODEX MAGAZINE
JOB APPLICATION

1. Position applied for: _____Editor_____   Today's date: _Nov. 12, 2010_

2. Full legal name _Skoap-Pohlig_____   _Nakisha_____   _Ann_____
                 Last   First   Middle

3. Current address _22 East 10th Street_____

   _Broadfield,_____   _Ohio_____   _43216_____   How long at this address? _5 months_____
       City   State   Zip Code

4. Previous address _17 Willow Terrace_____

   _Broadfield,_____   _Ohio_____   _43216_____   How long at this address? _1981–June 1, 2010_
       City   State   Zip Code

5. Education. Circle the number of years of post high school education. 1 2 3 4 5 6 ⑦ 8

6.

Name of Institution	Degree	Major	Dates Attended
1. _Claremont College_	B.A.	Journalism	2001–2005
2. _Ohio State University_	—	Urban Studies	2006
3. _Ohio State University_		Political Science	2008–present

   If you expect to complete an educational program soon, indicate the date and type of program.

   _I expect to receive my M.S. in political science in January_____

7. Current job. May we contact your present supervisor? _____ yes _×_ no

   Job Title _Reporter_____   Employer _Broadfield Examiner_____

   Type of Business _newspaper__   Address _1400 River Street, Broadfield, OH 43216___

   Dates (month/year) _9/2002___   to (month/year) _present_____

8. In your own handwriting, describe your duties and what you find most satisfying in this job.

   I am currently a crime reporter for a daily newspaper. I write local crime news.

   I especially enjoy working with my supervisor.

(continued on next page)

B. *Complete the personnel officer's notes. Use the correct affirmative or negative form of the verbs in parentheses—simple past, present perfect, or present perfect progressive. Sometimes there is more than one correct answer.*

1. I _have interviewed_ Nakisha Skoap-Pohlig for the editorial position.
   (interview)

2. She _____ for a job on November 12.
   (apply)

3. She _____ at the *Broadfield Examiner* for a long time.
   (work)

4. She _____ several excellent articles for that publication.
   (write)

5. She _____ that job while she _____ a college student.
   (find)   **(be)**

6. She _____ two schools of higher education.
   (attend)

7. She _____ classes at Claremont College in 2001 and _____ her
   (begin)   **(receive)**

   B.A. there.

8. Then she _____ to Ohio State University.
   (go on)

9. She _____ classes in two different departments at Ohio State.
   (take)

10. She _____ a master's program in urban studies.
    (start)

11. She _____ a degree in urban studies, though.
    (get)

12. After a year, she _____ to study political science instead.
    (decide)

13. She _____ her master's degree yet.
    (receive)

14. She _____ on Willow Terrace most of her life.
    (live)

15. For the past five months, she _____ on East 10th Street.
    (live)

16. In our recent conversations, the company graphologist _____ asking the
    (recommend)

    applicant to come in for another interview.

17. He says that in question 8 of the application, Ms. Skoap-Pohlig _____ a space
    (leave)

    between some words when she mentioned her supervisor.

18. He feels that this means she probably _____ her supervisor yet about looking
    (tell)

    for a new job.

19. When Ms. Skoap-Pohlig answered question 8, she _____ her writing to either
    (slant)

    the left or the right.

20. The graphologist _____ to me yesterday that this indicates that she is a clear
    (explain)

    and independent thinker.

Read the letter to an advice column. There are fourteen mistakes in the use of the simple past, present perfect, and present perfect progressive. The first mistake is already corrected. Find and correct thirteen more.

Dear John,

          been making

  My grandson and his girlfriend have ~~made~~ wedding plans for the past few months. At

first I was delighted, but last week I have heard something that changed my feelings. It

seems that our future granddaughter-in-law has been deciding to keep her own last name

after the wedding. Her reasons: First, she doesn't want to "lose her identity." Her parents

have named her 31 years ago, and she was Donna Esposito since then. She sees no reason

to change now. Second, she is a member of the Rockland Symphony Orchestra and she

performed with them for eight years. As a result, she already became known professionally

by her maiden name.

  John, when I've gotten married, I didn't think of keeping my maiden name. I have felt so

proud when I became "Mrs. Smith." We named our son after my father, but our surname

showed that we three were a family.

  I've been reading two articles on this topic, and I can now understand her decision to

use her maiden name professionally. But I still can't understand why she wants to use

it socially.

  My husband and I have been trying many times to hide our hurt feelings, but it's been

getting harder. I want to tell her and my grandson what I think, but I don't want to ruin

his wedding celebration.

  My grandson didn't say anything so far, so we don't know how he feels. Have we been

making the right choice by keeping quiet?

      A Concerned Grandmother Who Hasn't Been Saying One Word Yet

EXERCISE 5: Personal Writing

Write an email to a friend about a new interest or hobby that you have. Use some of the phrases from the box.

At first, I didn't . . .	I've just . . .
Before I . . .	One of the best things about . . .
For the past several weeks, . . .	Since I . . .
I still haven't . . .	You won't believe it. I've been . . .
I'm amazed that I've already . . .	

Past Perfect and Past Perfect Progressive

EXERCISE 1: Spelling: Regular and Irregular Past Participles

Write the correct forms of the verbs.

Base Form	Present Participle	Past Participle
1. bet	*betting*	*bet*
2. _____	breaking	_____
3. cut	_____	_____
4. do	_____	_____
5. entertain	_____	_____
6. _____	_____	fought
7. forgive	_____	_____
8. _____	leading	_____
9. plan	_____	_____
10. practice	_____	_____
11. quit	_____	_____
12. _____	_____	sought
13. _____	_____	sunk
14. steal	_____	_____
15. sweep	_____	_____
16. swim	_____	_____
17. _____	telling	_____
18. _____	_____	withdrawn

EXERCISE 2: Past Perfect: Affirmative and Negative Statements

Read the online article about Lang Lang. Complete the information with the affirmative or negative past perfect form of the verbs in parentheses.

○○○ www.WikiWonders.com

Music superstar Lang Lang was born in Shenyang, China in 1982. By the time he was three years old, he

___*had started*___ taking piano lessons. According
1. (start)

to Lang, he _____ Liszt's "Hungarian
2. (hear)

Rhapsody No. 2" during a *Tom and Jerry* cartoon, and

he _____ to play classical music, just
3. (decide)

like the music in the cartoon. By the time he was five,

Lang _____ first place in a major
4. (win)

competition, and his family _____ the importance of giving their son the best music
5. (realize)

education possible.

   After Lang Lang _____ on his piano skills for several years, he finally received
6. (work)

admission to the Central Conservatory of Music in Beijing. As a teenager, he took first prize in a

number of international competitions because he _____ an opportunity to study
7. (have)

with some of the best teachers in China and because he _____ a great love of music
8. (develop)

and a strong desire to be the best. But Lang _____ all of his goals yet. Before his
9. (reach)

sixteenth birthday, he _____ to the U.S. to study at the Curtis Institute of Music in
10. (move)

Philadelphia. Not long after, he began his professional career. By the time he turned twenty, Lang

_____ one of the most popular and successful concert pianists in the world.
11. (become)

   In 2008, Lang Lang's popularity increased when he played at the Opening Ceremony of the

Beijing Olympic Games. Many people in the audience _____ to classical music
12. (listen)

before. They were surprised at the beauty and excitement of his performance and were suddenly

fans. Interestingly, Lang Lang _____ to participate in the ceremony not just to
13. (agree)

represent his home country or become more famous. He _____ a sports fan since he
14. (be)

was a boy, so he enthusiastically performed, gave interviews, and attended events throughout the

Beijing Games. He also signed a contract with his favorite athletic equipment company and soon

---

began wearing Adidas Lang Lang Gazelle sneakers on stage. Because he _____

15. (bring)

sports, fashion, and his superstar quality to the serious works of composers such as Mozart, Liszt,

and Stravinsky, *Time* added Lang Lang to its list of the 100 Most Influential People in the World in

2009. According to the magazine, along with other talented young musicians, Lang Lang

_____ the world of classical music.

16. (transform)

For more on Lang Lang, visit www.langlang.com.

EXERCISE 3: Past Perfect: *Yes / No* Questions and Short Answers

Look at the musician's busy schedule. Complete the questions about his day and give short answers. Use the past perfect.

1. It was 6:00 A.M.

A: _____ *Had he gotten up yet?* _____

B: _____ *Yes, he had.* _____

2. The young musician was taking his morning jog.

A: _____ piano yet?

B: _____

3. It was 11:00 A.M

A: _____ with

reporters by then?

B: _____

4. It was noon.

A: _____ his

parents yet?

B: _____

5. It was shortly before 6:00 P.M.

A: _____ his warm-up exercises?

B: _____

Today	
A.M.	
5:00	get up
6:00	take a jog in the park
8:00	practice piano
10:00	meet with news reporters
10:30	play Ping-Pong to relax
P.M.	
12:00	have lunch
3:00	call parents
6:00	do warm-up exercises for concert
7:00	start performance
10:30	check the following day's schedule
11:00	go to bed

(continued on next page)

6. It was 7:30 P.M.

A: _____ that evening's performance?

B: _____

7. At 11:00 P.M., he went to bed.

A: _____ the following day's schedule?

B: _____

EXERCISE 4: Past Perfect Progressive: Affirmative and Negative Statements

Read the situations. Draw conclusions, using the affirmative or negative past perfect progressive form of the correct verbs from the box.

cry	drink	laugh	pay	wash
do	eat	listen	rain	~~watch~~

1. Mara wasn't in the living room, but her DVD player was on.

She _____ *had been watching* _____ *Tom and Jerry* cartoons.

2. The lights were off, and none of her schoolbooks were around.

She _____ homework.

3. The window was open, and the floor was a little wet.

It _____.

4. There was half a sandwich on the coffee table.

Mara _____ the sandwich.

5. There was an unopened bottle of soda next to the sandwich.

She _____ the soda.

6. Mara came into the living room. There were tears on her face.

At first I thought she _____.

7. I was wrong. Mara wasn't upset.

She _____ really hard because of what was happening in

one of the cartoons.

8. There was a stack of clean plates next to the kitchen sink.

   She _____ dishes.

9. Mara could hear the TV from the kitchen.

   She _____ to the cartoons from the kitchen.

10. I was surprised when I realized how late it was.

    I _____ attention to the time.

EXERCISE 5: Past Perfect Progressive: Questions

A student reporter from a university newspaper is researching some background information before his interview with a famous musician. Use **when** *and the words in parentheses to write his research questions. Use the past perfect progressive.*

1. He recorded his first successful CD. (he / dream of stardom for a long time)

   Had he been dreaming of stardom for a long time when he recorded his first successful CD?

2. He finally received a recording contract. (How long / he / live in New York)

   _____

3. He got his first job as a musician. (he / really work as a cook in a fast-food restaurant)

   _____

4. He decided to enroll at the Berklee School of Music. (Where / he / study)

   _____

5. He began his music classes. (Why / he / take courses in accounting)

   _____

6. He realized he wanted to be a professional musician. (How long / he / play piano)

   _____

7. He established his new scholarship program. (he / look for ways to help young musicians for a

   long time)

   _____

Complete the article. Use the past perfect or past perfect progressive form of the verbs in parentheses. Use the progressive form when possible.

A Pop Music Sensation

In 2009, American R&B singer Beyoncé Knowles had a worldwide hit with her "Single Ladies"

video. But that was not her first success. The talented young star __had been performing__ since
1. (perform)

she was a girl. Before they were teens, she and several of her friends _____ to
2. (begin)

sing professionally. By that time, she _____ music and dance for several years.
3. (study)

Beyoncé got interested in singing after she

_____ first prize in a talent contest in her
4. (receive)

school for her version of John Lennon's song, "Imagine." Before the

contest, her dance instructor _____ Beyoncé's
5. (hear)

incredible voice, and she _____ her student to
6. (push)

develop all of her skills. In 1997, Beyoncé _____
7. (be)

a singer-dancer for a decade when she signed a contract with

Columbia Records and became successful as a member of Destiny's

Child. She was just sixteen years old. By the time the group made its final appearance together

in 2006, Beyoncé _____ as a solo artist for some time. Since 2001, she
8. (work)

_____ in Hollywood movies, and of course she _____
9. (star)   **10. (record)**

music. She _____ a top-selling album, and in 2004 her fans got what they
11. (have)

_____ for when she won five Grammy Awards in a single night. Beyoncé's
12. (wait)

popularity continued to grow with more albums, more movies, and more awards—both before

and after "Single Ladies."

Look at some important events in Beyoncé Knowles's life and career. Determine the correct order of the phrases. Then combine the phrases and use the past perfect or past perfect progressive to express the event that happened first. Use the progressive form when possible. Use the simple past for the event that happened second. Add commas when necessary.

The Life and Times of Beyoncé Knowles

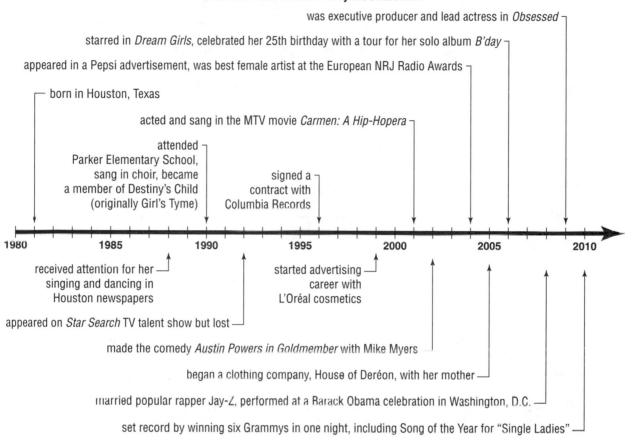

1. attended Parker Elementary School / received attention in Houston newspapers

   Before *Beyoncé attended Parker Elementary School, she had received attention in*

   Houston newspapers.

2. lost the *Star Search* competition / signed a contract with Columbia records

   After _____

   _____

3. work at Columbia Records for several years / was in an ad for L'Oréal cosmetics

   _____

   by the time _____

(continued on next page)

4. filmed an MTV movie / made the comedy *Austin Powers in Goldmember*

Beyoncé _____

after _____

5. sang in a Pepsi ad / did ads for L'Oréal

When _____

already _____

6. start a clothing company with her mother / celebrated her 25th birthday

By the time _____

_____

7. acted for five years / starred in *Dream Girls*

_____

when _____

8. got married to Jay-Z / become internationally famous

_____

before _____

9. finish the movie *Obsessed* / performed at a Barack Obama presidential celebration

When _____

already _____

10. set a record by winning six Grammy awards in one night / earned millions from recording, movie, and advertising contracts

By the time _____

already _____

EXERCISE 8: Editing

Read the review of a concert a student wrote for her school newspaper. There are ten mistakes in the use of the past perfect and past perfect progressive. The first mistake is already corrected. Find and correct nine more.

My assignment for tonight was to see Lang Lang at Symphony Center. To be honest, I hadn't

expected much before I ~~had gone~~ *went* to the concert. In fact, I hadn't been look forward to it at all.

But then Lang Lang got my attention with his first two pieces.

By intermission, I had totally change my mind. Lang Lang had played just "Hungarian

Rhapsody No. 2," and the audience had gone wild. I had been hearing Lizst's composition many

times before, but not like that. By the time he finishes playing, everyone in the audience had

jumped to their feet and had started clapping enthusiastically. And the best part of the concert

had started yet.

After intermission, Lang Lang invited several young musicians to join him on the stage. All of

them had been winning a scholarship from the Lang Lang International Music Foundation. When

each child performed, I had felt their excitement and their passion for music. It was wonderful to

see that talented children could have a chance to succeed, regardless of their ethnic

background or financial situation.

Superstar quality was certainly on display tonight. As I left Symphony Center, I had to ask

myself a question. Lang Lang was absolutely incredible. Why I had taken so long to find out

about him?

EXERCISE 9: Personal Writing

On a separate piece of paper, write a paragraph about an experience that surprised you. Tell what you did. Then explain how the experience changed the way you thought and felt. Use some of the phrases from the box.

Afterwards, . . .	I had an interesting experience . . .
As soon as . . .	I had never . . . before . . .
By the time it ended . . .	It happened . . .
I changed my opinion because . . .	When it started . . .
I had always . . . but . . .	

UNIT 5 Future and Future Progressive

EXERCISE 1: Contrast of Future Forms

Circle the best words to complete the conversation between two friends.

1. A: Hi, Toni. Are you busy?

   B: Yes, I'm packing. Victor and I have plans. <u>We'll go / (We're going)</u> out of town tomorrow.

2. A: Do you need a bigger suitcase?

   B: Actually, I do.

   A: OK. <u>I'm going to bring / I'll bring</u> one over right away.

3. A: <u>Do you take / Are you taking</u> your dog on the trip?

   B: No. We can't. It's a business trip.

4. A: Your poor dog! <u>He's going to miss / He's missing</u> you.

   B: I know, but <u>we won't be / we aren't</u> out of town long.

5. A: So, give me some details about the trip.

   B: <u>We're attending / We'll attend</u> a World Future Society conference.

   A: When <u>does the conference start / will the conference start</u>?

   B: At 8:30 on Tuesday morning.

6. A: The phone is ringing.

   B: It's probably Victor. <u>I'll answer / I'm going to answer</u> it.

7. A: Watch out! The phone is on the edge of the table. <u>It'll fall / It's going to fall</u>.

   B: Relax. I have everything under control.

8. A: What are your plans for the conference?

   B: <u>We'll see / We're going to see</u> several presentations on Masdar City in the United Arab

      Emirates. Victor really wants to get a new job there, but he keeps promising me that

      <u>he won't apply / he isn't going to apply</u> for the job until we get more information.

9. A: I have to finish packing. <u>Our plane will leave / Our plane leaves</u> at 6:30 A.M.

B: What? You've already completely filled my largest suitcase, and just look at the zipper.

<u>It'll break / It's going to break</u>.

EXERCISE 2: Future Progressive: Affirmative and Negative Statements

Complete the article. Use the affirmative or negative future progressive form of the words in parentheses.

A Green City in the Desert

If all goes according to plan, as many as 50,000 people

_____ *will be living* _____ in super green[1] Masdar City in
1. (will / live)
the United Arab Emirates in 2020. Amazingly, residents

_____ the comforts of modern life, but
2. (will / enjoy)
they _____ the environment.
3. (will / harm)

Although Masdar City will be located in one of the richest oil countries in the world, its

citizens _____ fossil fuel. They _____
4. (be going to / use)   **5. (be going to / take advantage of)**
the sun and the wind as sources of power in their zero-carbon, zero-waste community.

Construction is already underway on Masdar City. In the coming years, architects and

engineers _____ on creative ways to make this green city a reality.
6. (will / work)
At the same time, graduate students at the Masdar Institute of Science and Technology

_____ research to develop innovative products and construction
7. (be going to / do)
techniques to meet the challenges of this exciting project.

One of the biggest challenges for any green community is transportation. The residents of

Masdar City _____. In fact, there will be no cars. People
8. (will / drive)
_____ in small electric vehicles that will be part of the public
9. (be going to / travel)
transportation system. Even better, they _____. After all, the
10. (will / walk)
_____

[1]*green:* a. the color green (because of trees and plants) b. protective of the environment

(continued on next page)

streets of Masdar City will have protection from the sun and hot temperatures of the desert, and

with new technology, cool air _____ in from the nearby Persian Gulf.
                                      11. (be going to / blow)

Speaking of water, residents of Masdar City _____ water from
                                                  12. (will / drink)

the Persian Gulf after the salt is removed from it in a solar powered plant. Then, additional

technology _____ the waste water so that it can be used for
              13. (be going to / clean)

farming and other purposes. And that's not all. When Masdar City is complete, it will be

totally waste-free. Workers _____ garbage to create power, and
                                14. (will / burn)

they _____ materials for reuse and recycling.
      15. (will / collect)

It will cost approximately $22 billion to build Masdar City, and the government of Abu

Dhabi _____ most of the bills. Officials there see it as smart
        16. (will / pay)

planning. If futurists are correct, more and more countries _____
                                                                17. (be going to / try)

to follow the model of this eco-city in the desert sometime soon.

EXERCISE 3: Future Progressive: Questions and Short Answers

Complete the conversations. Use the future progressive form of the words in parentheses or
short answers where appropriate.

1. **A:** When _will you be making your decision_____?
                                          (you / will / make your decision)
   B: Tomorrow. It won't take long for us to decide who will be getting the job.

2. **A:** _____?
            (the company / will / pay for my wife's airfare)
   B: _____. Any job offer we give will include airline tickets for

   your entire family to Abu Dhabi.

3. **A:** Toni, _____?
                  (you / be going to / travel alone)
   B: _____. Victor and I are going to be on the same flight.

4. **A:** You're leaving so soon! Between now and the day you leave for Victor's new job, what

   _____?
                              (you / be going to / do)
   B: I have a lot of things to take care of, but we'll have time to go out for lunch. I promise.

5. A: Victor, _____?
(you / will / stop at the consulate office today)

   B: _____. The Masdar company assistant is taking care of all our

     travel documents. She's great.

6. A: _____?
(she / be going to / send the travel documents soon)

   B: _____. I expect everything to arrive in the next couple of days.

7. A: What kind of apartment _____?
(we / will / live in)

   B: Hey, stop worrying. Everything will be great in Masdar City. You'll love it.

8. A: How _____?
(we / will / get to the airport)

   B: I think that we should take a taxi.

EXERCISE 4: Future Progressive or Simple Present

*Look at Toni's and Victor's schedules for tomorrow. Complete the statements. Use the correct form of the verbs—future progressive with **will** or simple present.*

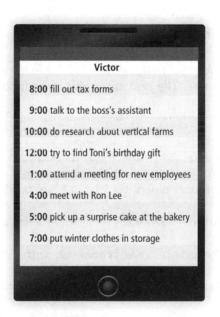

Toni		Victor	
8:00 go to the post office		**8:00** fill out tax forms	
9:00 call the electric company		**9:00** talk to the boss's assistant	
10:00 buy everything on the shopping list		**10:00** do research about vertical farms	
12:00 eat lunch with Aidiya		**12:00** try to find Toni's birthday gift	
1:00 visit Mom		**1:00** attend a meeting for new employees	
4:00 take the dog to Brigitte's house		**4:00** meet with Ron Lee	
5:00 prepare dinner		**5:00** pick up a surprise cake at the bakery	
7:00 finish packing		**7:00** put winter clothes in storage	

1. While Toni _____*goes to*_____ the post office,

    Victor _____*will be filling out tax forms*_____ for his new job.

2. Victor _____ his boss's assistant

    while Toni _____.

(continued on next page)

3. Toni _____ on her shopping list before the trip to Masdar City,

while Victor _____.

4. While Victor _____

Toni _____ with Aidiya.

5. Victor _____

while Toni _____ her mother.

6. While Victor _____ with Ron Lee,

Toni _____.

7. Victor _____ at the bakery

while Toni _____.

8. While Toni _____,

Victor _____ in storage.

EXERCISE 5: Editing

Read Victor's journal entry. Victor has made ten mistakes in the use of the future and the future progressive. The first mistake is already corrected. Find and correct nine more.

>   *I'm going*
> It's 11:00 P.M. now. ~~I go~~ to bed in a few minutes, but I'm afraid that I won't
> get much sleep tonight. I'll be tired when I will get up, but I can't stop thinking
> about my new job. Toni has our last day here completely planned. In the morning,
> we're going have breakfast with friends and family. Then we're taking care of
> a few last-minute errands. Our plane will leave at 5:00 P.M., and Toni has
> already made a reservation for a taxi at 2:00. I'm really excited. At this time
> tomorrow, Toni and I will be sit on the airplane on our way to Abu Dhabi. If I
> know Toni, she is enjoying a movie while I will try to catch up on my sleep. Oh,
> no, I hear thunder. It will rain, so I'd better close all the windows. Maybe I'm
> going to watch the rain for a while. It's a long time before I see rain again.

EXERCISE 6: Personal Writing

Write a paragraph about a trip that you are planning. Use some of the phrases from the box.

Before I return home . . .	The best part of the trip will . . .
During the first part of the trip . . .	When I get back . . .
One day soon, I am going . . .	While I . . . , all my friends back home will be . . .
One thing is for sure. On this trip, I won't be . . .	While I'm there . . .

Future Perfect and Future Perfect Progressive

EXERCISE 1: Affirmative and Negative Statements

Complete the article. Use the affirmative or negative future perfect form of the words in parentheses.

As of January next year, Pam and Jessica Weiner, two sisters
_____ *will have taught* _____ dozens of
                            1. (teach)
personal management seminars to grateful clients. Tired of
disorganization in their own homes, Pam and Jessica developed a
system that worked so well that they started teaching it to others. By
this anniversary celebration, hundreds of people across the country
_____ the Weiners' seminars, and these efficient
                    2. (take)
sisters _____ them manage the confusion and
                            3. (help)
stress in their lives.

   "What a difference their seminars made!" exclaimed Terrie Smith, who completed the course
two years ago. "By the end of November, I _____
                                                            4. (use)
the system to complete my holiday shopping. I _____
                                                            5. (purchase)
all my gifts, and I _____ them too. I'll actually
                            6. (wrap)
have time to enjoy the holidays this year."

   Why do we need a time-management system? According to Pam Weiner, statistics show that
people are extremely busy these days. For most of us, it seems that there are not enough hours
in the day, so we need to budget our time. Weiner gave an example of a new family in their
seminar. She said, "Ana and Jon are busy with their two children, and they both work.
However, they have no system, and this creates stress. By next Monday, the busy couple

_____ the week's menu yet, and they
7. (plan)

_____ on a driving schedule for the week's
8. (decide)

activities, which will cause a lot of problems. By the time Friday comes along, it is likely that

they _____ more than once about these things.
9. (argue)

As a result, they will feel frustrated, angry, and tired."

The Metcalfs, one of many satisfied families, agree. As Aida Metcalf explained, "At the end

of this week, we _____ a lot in a minimum
10. (accomplish)

amount of time, and we _____ our energy
11. (waste)

arguing about who does what in the house. Even better, because of our plan we

_____ all the housework by noon on Saturday
12. (finish)

and we can make plans to go out. Then, when we go back to work on Monday morning, we

_____ a good time for part of the weekend, and
13. (have)

we'll feel refreshed and ready to start a new week."

In the Metcalfs' experience, the time-management system also works well for long-range

planning. Aida said, "Before our seminar with the Weiners, our summers were a nightmare. We

never got to do the things we really wanted to do. But by the end of August this year, we

_____ in our community yardsale, and
14. (participate)

_____ the house. What's more, we
15. (redecorate)

_____ all the preparations for our annual
16. (make)

September family get-together."

Pam and Jessica Weiner will celebrate another anniversary when they are guests once again

on tomorrow's broadcast of *Around Town*. "Our television appearances started with this

show," Pam pointed out. "As of tomorrow, we _____
17. (explain)

our system to television audiences each Friday for an entire year."

EXERCISE 2: Questions and Answers

Look at the Metcalfs' calendar for August. Write questions and answers about their activities. Use the future perfect.

AUGUST

SUNDAY	MONDAY	TUESDAY	WEDNESDAY	THURSDAY	FRIDAY	SATURDAY
1 Aida walk 1/2 mi every day	**2** Arnie paint first bedroom	**3** Arnie paint second bedroom	**4** Arnie paint bathroom	**5** Aida start driving in carpool for day camp	**6**	**7**
8 Aida water garden daily	**9** Corrie and Marsha pick vegetables daily	**10**	**11** Arnie paint downstairs	**12**	**13**	**14** Arnie put furniture back after painting
15	**16** Arnie 4:00 P.M. dentist appointment	**17** Arnie meet with banker to discuss ways to become debt-free	**18** Corrie pick blueberries for pies (need 3 quarts)	**19** Aida start baking pies for bake sale (agreed to bring 6 pies)	**20** Aida call Arnie's sister	**21** Community Center bake sale
22 Aida start unpacking fall clothing	**23** Arnie plan menu for family get-together	**24**	**25** Iron and put away fall clothing	**26** Last day of summer camp for Corrie and Marsha	**27**	**28** Arnie go shopping
29 Aida and Arnie pack for trip to Mom and Dad's	**30** Aida pay credit card bills	**31** Family travel to Aunt Irene's house				

1. (How many miles / Aida / walk / by August 31)

   A: How many miles will Aida have walked by August 31?

   B: She'll have walked 15.5 miles.

2. (Arnie / paint the bathroom / by August 5)

   A: Will Arnie have painted the bathroom by August 5?

   B: Yes, he will.

3. (How many rooms / Arnie / paint / by August 5)

A: _____

B: _____

4. (When / Arnie / finish all the painting)

A: _____

B: _____

5. (Aida / start driving the carpool / by August 6)

A: _____

B: _____

6. (on August 16 / Arnie / leave / for his dentist appointment / by 4:00)

A: _____

B: _____

7. (Aida / unpack / all the fall clothing / by August 23)

A: _____

B: _____

8. (How many quarts of blueberries / Corrie / pick / by August 19)

A: _____

B: _____

9. (How many pies / Aida / bake / by August 21)

A: _____

B: _____

10. (they / finish / packing for the trip / by August 31)

A: _____

B: _____

EXERCISE 3: Future Perfect Progressive and Time Clauses

Look at the Metcalfs' August calendar again. Complete the statements. Use the simple present and future perfect or future perfect progressive. Use the future perfect progressive when possible.

1. By the time ___Aida begins driving in the carpool_____,
   (begin driving in the carpool)
   _____Arnie will have been painting_____ for several days.
   (paint)

2. When _____,
   (start the family get-together menu)
   _____ for a couple of weeks.
   (pick vegetables)

3. _____
   (call Arnie's sister)
   before _____.
   (do the menu)

4. _____ already
   (meet with the family's banker)
   when _____.
   (pay the monthly credit card bills)

5. By the time _____,
   (finish the fall clothes)
   _____ for four days.
   (work on them)

6. When _____ on August 21,
   (takes place)
   _____ yet.
   (finish summer camp)

7. _____ for almost a week
   (plan his special menu)
   by the time _____.
   (go shopping)

8. By the time _____,
   (travel to Aunt Irene's house)
   _____.
   (have a very productive month)

EXERCISE 4: Editing

Read the electronic ad. There are eight mistakes in the use of the future perfect and future perfect progressive. The first mistake is already corrected. Find and correct seven more.

EXERCISE 5: Personal Writing

Make a list of ten things you hope to accomplish by the end of the class(es) that you are now taking. Put them in order of importance—from least important to most important. Use some of the phrases from the box.

By the time . . .	Most importantly, I will . . .
I will . . . before . . .	This class will end _____. By then, I . . .
I will have been . . . so I . . .	When the class is over, I will already . . .
If all goes according to plan, I will . . .	

PART III

NEGATIVE QUESTIONS, TAG QUESTIONS, ADDITIONS AND RESPONSES

UNIT 7 Negative *Yes / No* Questions and Tag Questions

EXERCISE 1: Affirmative and Negative Tag Questions and Short Answers

Anne-Marie wants to rent an apartment. Complete her conversation with the landlord. Use appropriate tags. Write short answers based on the apartment ad.

> N. Smithfield unfurn. 1 BR in owner occup. bldg.,
> renovated kitchen w. all new appliances, incl.
> DW, near all transp. & shopping, $750/mo. + util.
> Avail. for immed. occup. Pets OK. 555-7738

1. **ANNE-MARIE:** _The rent is $750, isn't it?_

   LANDLORD: _Yes, it is._

2. **ANNE-MARIE:** That includes electricity, _____

   LANDLORD: _____

3. **ANNE-MARIE:** The apartment isn't furnished, _____

   LANDLORD: _____

4. **ANNE-MARIE:** You've renovated the original kitchen, _____

   LANDLORD: _____

5. **ANNE-MARIE:** The kitchen doesn't have a dishwasher, _____

   LANDLORD: _____

6. **ANNE-MARIE:** You just put in a new refrigerator, _____

   LANDLORD: _____

7. **ANNE-MARIE:** A bus stops nearby, _____

   LANDLORD: _____

8. ANNE-MARIE: I can't move in right away, _____

   LANDLORD: _____

9. ANNE-MARIE: My pets won't bother you, _____

   LANDLORD: _____

10. ANNE-MARIE: You live right in the building, _____

   LANDLORD: _____

EXERCISE 2: Negative *Yes* / *No* Questions and Short Answers

*Todd and a realtor are discussing two communities—North Smithfield and Greenwood. Complete their conversation. Use negative **yes** / **no** questions to ask about Greenwood. Write short answers based on the information in the box.*

> ### Greenwood—Community Profile
>
> Greenwood became a town in 1782. It has a number of historic buildings.
> **Schools:** Greenwood High School, Greenwood Community College
> **Shopping:** Greenwood Mall
> **Transportation:** local public bus
> **Recreational Facilities:** Briar State Park, Greenwood Beach (private),
> Davis Baseball Stadium (planned for next year)
> **Cultural Opportunities:** movie theaters (Greenwood Mall)
> **Average Rent:** $795

1. REALTOR: North Smithfield has a community college.

   TODD: *Doesn't Greenwood have a community college?* _____

   REALTOR: *Yes, it does.* _____

2. REALTOR: North Smithfield built a public beach.

   TODD: _____

   REALTOR: _____

3. REALTOR: There are historic structures in North Smithfield.

   TODD: _____

   REALTOR: _____

(continued on next page)

4. REALTOR: You can see live theater performances in North Smithfield.

TODD: _____

REALTOR: _____

5. REALTOR: People in North Smithfield shop at a nearby mall.

TODD: _____

REALTOR: _____

6. REALTOR: The average rent in North Smithfield is under $800.

TODD: _____

REALTOR: _____

7. REALTOR: North Smithfield has been a town for more than a hundred years.

TODD: _____

REALTOR: _____

8. REALTOR: They're going to build a baseball stadium in North Smithfield.

TODD: _____

REALTOR: _____

EXERCISE 3: Negative *Yes / No* Questions and Tag Questions

Complete the conversations. Use the correct form of the verbs in parentheses. Write negative **yes / no** *questions and tag questions.*

A.   ARI: _____*Didn't*_____ you _____*move in*_____ last week?
                                                    1. (move in)

DAN: Yes. You haven't been living here very long yourself, _____*have you*_____?
                                                                              2.

ARI: Oh, it's been about a year now.

DAN: It's a nice place to live, _____?
                                              3.

ARI: We think so. We adjusted very quickly when we moved here.

B.   KATIE: You haven't seen the letter carrier this morning, _____?
                                                                              1.

DAN: No. Why?

KATIE: I don't think our mail is being forwarded from our old address.

DAN: _____ you _____ one of those
                                              2. (fill out)

change-of-address forms that the post office provides?

KATIE: Yes. But that was almost a month ago. We should be getting our mail by now,

_____?
                    3.

DAN: I would think so.

C. **DAN:** _____ there an all-night supermarket nearby?
                        1. (be)

MIA: Yes. It's at 10th and Walnut.

DAN: I know where that is. _____ there _____
                                                                2. (used to / be)

a restaurant there?

MIA: That's right. It closed last year.

DAN: That's strange. It hadn't been there very long, _____?
                                                                        3.

MIA: About a year. I guess the location just didn't attract much business.

D. **ARI:** The new neighbors are really friendly, _____?
                                                                1.

MIA: Yes. That reminds me. The people across the hall invited us over for coffee and cake on

Saturday afternoon. You haven't made any plans for then, _____?
                                                                                    2.

ARI: Well, I was going to work on our taxes.

MIA: _____ you _____ a little break?
                                        3. (can / take)

ARI: Sure. Why not?

EXERCISE 4: Negative *Yes / No* Questions and Tag Questions

The new tenants are going to visit their neighbors. They want to confirm some of the assumptions they have. Read their assumptions. Then write negative **yes** / **no** *questions or tag questions. For some sentences, both types of questions are possible. (Remember: The only time you can use negative* **yes** / **no** *questions is when you think the answer is "Yes.")*

1. We think the people in Apartment 4F have lived here a long time.

 The people in Apartment 4F have lived here a long time, haven't they? OR _____

 Haven't the people in Apartment 4F lived here a long time? _____

2. I don't think our apartment had been occupied for a while.

 Our apartment hadn't been occupied for a while, had it? _____

3. We believe this is a good building.

 _____

(continued on next page)

4. It seems that the owner takes good care of it.

_____

5. It looks like he has just finished renovations on the lobby.

_____

6. We don't think that he painted our apartment before we moved in.

_____

7. I have the impression he doesn't talk very much.

_____

8. I don't think the rent will increase next year.

_____

9. It looks like some new people will be moving into Apartment 1B.

_____

10. We have the impression that this is a really nice place to live.

_____

EXERCISE 5: Editing

Two students are preparing a role-play for English class. The lesson is about problems getting an apartment. There are ten mistakes with negative **yes** / **no** questions and tag questions in the dialogue. The first one is already corrected. Find and correct nine more.

                                                    don't

MARIAM: You own this building, ~~didn't~~ you?

OWNER: Yes. And you've been living next door for about a year now, have you?

MARIAM: That's right. But I'm interested in moving. There's a vacant apartment in your

building, isn't it?

OWNER: Yes. It's a one-bedroom on the fourth floor. The rent is $900 a month, plus utilities.

MARIAM: Wow! That's a lot of money, isn't it? Could you not lower the rent a little?

OWNER: Wait a minute! You came over here to talk to me, haven't you? You want to live here,

don't you?

MARIAM: No. I love this building. It would be perfect for me, but I can't pay $900 a month.

OWNER: But this is an historic structure. I was originally planning to charge $1,000 a month.

MARIAM: I know. The history is what attracted me in the first place. But the elevator isn't working, isn't it?

OWNER: No, it isn't. OK, so if I lower the rent, you'll do some things in the apartment like painting, won't they?

MARIAM: Definitely. And I'm going to pay $700 a month, amn't I?

OWNER: OK, OK. And you can move in next weekend, can you?

MARIAM: It's a deal!

EXERCISE 6: Personal Writing

Write questions about the place where you live, study, or work. Then find someone who will answer the questions for you. Use negative **yes / no** *questions and tag questions to confirm information you think you already know. Use some of the phrases from the box.*

. . . , are they?	. . . , don't they?	Isn't this . . . ?
. . . , aren't I?	Doesn't this building . . . ?	There are a lot of . . . ?
. . . , can it?	Haven't . . . ?	We won't . . . ?

Additions and Responses:
So, Too, Neither, Not either, and *But*

Read the true story about twin sisters. Circle the correct words to complete the story.

Mirror, Mirror, on the Wall

Olga and Carmen Landa have gotten a lot of attention since they were infants. In fact, they remember being treated like rock stars in the small town in Venezuela where they grew up. It's no coincidence that people have always been interested in them because Olga and Carmen are mirror-image twins.

Mirror-image twins are identical, but they have opposite physical characteristics, personality traits, and preferences. For example, Olga writes with her left hand, but Carmen (doesn't)/ didn't.
1.
She's right-handed. Olga is outgoing and relaxed about life, but Carmen isn't / doesn't. She is
2.
very serious about making plans and getting things done as quickly as possible. According to the sisters, Carmen has always been very organized and very neat, but Olga has / hasn't. Olga says
3.
that she doesn't mind if things are a little on the messy side. Olga has a strong fashion identity, and so / too does Carmen. Olga doesn't like extreme styles. Neither / So does her sister, but
4. **5.**
that's where the similarities end. Olga is the sporty twin who prefers pants and comfortable shoes, while Carmen wears skirts and high heels. Olga will buy clothes that are black or brightly colored, but her sister will / won't. Her favorite colors are white or earth-tones like brown, beige,
6.
and yellow.

Being mirror-image twins doesn't take away from the strong connection that Olga and Carmen feel. Olga can't imagine a life without her sister, and / but Carmen can't neither / either.
7. **8.**
The two of them are best friends who have always been a pair. They studied together during elementary school, high school, and university. After they worked for a few years, Carmen

decided to come to the U.S. to pursue her career in psychology. So <u>did Olga / Olga did</u>. It seems

9.

that when one of them gets an idea, the other one does <u>too / either</u>. If you ask them, the sisters

10.

will tell you they have always been the same, but always different.

EXERCISE 2: Affirmative or Negative?

Complete the conversations with affirmative and negative additions and responses.

A. KALEB: I've heard that there's a twins festival every year.

    KAREN: _____*So have*_____ I.
                  1.

    KALEB: I didn't realize that there were enough twins around to have a festival.

    KAREN: I _____. But hundreds of them attended the festival last year.
                     2.

    KALEB: I'm talking about the festival in Twinsburg, Ohio.

    KAREN: I _____. Did you know that some of the people who go there actually fall
                     3.

        in love and get married?

    KALEB: Are you kidding?

    KAREN: No. In 1998, Diane Sanders and her twin sister Darlene went to the festival in Twinsburg,

        and Craig Sanders and his brother Mark _____. Diane and Craig fell in
                                   4.

        love, and _____ Darlene and Mark.
                  5.

    KALEB: Let me guess. Their children are twins.

    KAREN: Not exactly. Diane and Craig have identical twin sons, _____ Darlene and

        Mark _____. They have two singletons—one daughter was born in 2001
                   6.

        and the other in 2003.

    KALEB: What's a singleton?

    KAREN: A child that isn't a twin.

B. ELLIE: I thought I knew where the expression "Siamese twins" came from, _____

        I _____. I had to look it up.
               1.

    GRANT: What did you find out?

(continued on next page)

ELLIE: Well, you know it refers to identical twins whose bodies are joined. Chang and Eng Bunker were conjoined twins who were born in Siam in 1811. The term was originally used to describe them. The preferred term today is "conjoined twins."

GRANT: I remember reading about them. Most doctors at the time had never seen conjoined twins, and _____ anyone else. Chang and Eng became famous.
2.

ELLIE: It's interesting. They ended up living in the United States. Chang got married, and _____ Eng. Their wives were sisters. Chang and his wife had 10 children,
3.

and Eng and his wife had 11.

GRANT: Do you know how they died?

ELLIE: When they were older, Chang was sick, _____ Eng _____.
4.

He was still strong and healthy. One night, Eng woke up, and his brother was dead. Eng died the same night.

C.   **KIM:** More and more women in the United States are having children later in life.

AMY: Women in Europe _____. The average age of new mothers is rising there.
1.

KIM: Because of the fact that new mothers are older and because of fertility treatments, the number of triplets, quadruplets, and quintuplets will continue to increase.

AMY: And _____ the number of twins.
2.

Look at the information about twins festivals. Then complete the sentences about the festivals. Use the information in parentheses to write appropriate additions and responses.

Twins Festivals			
LOCATION	**Twinsburg, Ohio, U.S.A**	**Pleucadeuc, France**	**Beijing, China**
YEAR STARTED	1976	1994	2004
TIME OF YEAR	first week of August	mid-August	first week of October
WHO ATTENDS	twins, triplets, quads, quints, and their families	twins, triplets, quads, quints, and their families	twins and the general public
TYPES OF EVENTS	talent show, parade, contests, food, fireworks, photos	music, parade, photographs, food	entertainment, social events
COST	$15, additional costs for triplets, quads, and quints	free	free
REGISTRATION	recommended	recommended	none required

and so does Pleucadeuc OR

1. Twinsburg, Ohio, has a twins festival each year, ___ *and Pleucadeuc does too* ___.
   (Pleucadeuc)

2. Twinsburg was holding its festival in the 1980s, _____.
   (Pleucadeuc)

3. Pleucadeuc doesn't charge an entrance fee, _____.
   (Beijing)

4. The Twinsburg festival isn't free, _____.
   (the Pleucadeuc and Beijing festivals)

5. Twinsburg will celebrate its festival next year, _____.
   (Pleucadeuc)

6. Twinsburg festival participants should register, _____.
   (participants at Pleucadeuc)

7. The Pleucadeuc festival doesn't have a talent show, _____.
   (the Beijing festival)

8. Twinsburg schedules its festival for August, _____.
   (Pleucadeuc)

9. Twins pay $15 at the Twinsburg festival, _____.
   (triplets, quads, and quints)

10. Pleucadeuc didn't sponsor a festival in 1990, _____.
    (Beijing)

11. Twins have gone to the Twinsburg festival for many years, _____.
    (their families)

EXERCISE 4: Editing

Read the online travel review. There are eight mistakes with additions and responses. The first one is already corrected. Find and correct seven more.

On the Road Reviews

Twins Days Festival ★ ★ ★ ★ ★

Twinsburg, OH

   Twinsburg really knows how to throw a party! I went to the festival in 2010. My twin sister and
                                    did
my cousins ~~do~~ too. We had a great time. I really enjoyed the line dancing, and so did my sister. I

had never done that kind of dancing before, but once I started, I couldn't stop, and neither can she.

To be honest, I was hoping to see a cute guy twin at the dance, and my sister did too, but we were

out of luck. I didn't meet anyone, and my sister didn't neither. But we still had fun. Our favorite

part was the picnic on Friday night. I loved seeing all the other twins there, and did my sister too.

   I have always liked being a twin, but my sister has. The Twinsburg festival changed all that. By

Saturday morning, she was really excited. Of course I was too. We couldn't wait for the

Double-Take Parade to start. My sister and I both marched in the parade. I felt really proud and

excited to be a part of it. So she did.

   Attending the Twins Day Festival with my sister may be a factor in why I liked it so much, but

my cousins aren't twins, and they can't wait to go back. My sister and I think the festival is

fantastic, and they are too.

EXERCISE 5: Personal Writing

On a separate piece of paper, write one or two paragraphs about yourself and the friend or family member that you resemble most. Use some of the phrases from the box.

Another similarity is . . .	The person that I resemble most is . . .
. . . does too.	We are really alike in . . .
. . . isn't either.	We have a lot in common. For example, . . .
Our greatest similarity is . . .	When I think about all that we have in common . . .

UNIT 9 Gerunds and Infinitives: Review and Expansion

EXERCISE 1: Gerund or Infinitive?

Complete the statements with the correct form—gerund or infinitive—of the verb **watch**. (Note: In some cases, both the infinitive and the gerund will be correct.)

1. The children wanted _____to watch_____ television.

2. I suggest _____watching_____ television.

3. We would like _____ television.

4. Do you need _____ television?

5. I was busy, so I really couldn't afford _____ television.

6. I should have stopped, but I continued _____ television.

7. Has a teacher ever encouraged you _____ television?

8. Some people dislike _____ television.

9. Others absolutely refuse _____ television.

10. Please turn off all the lights after you finish _____ television.

11. What time did you start _____ television?

12. My sister is addicted. She can't help _____ television.

13. How long ago did you quit _____ television?

14. Do you mind _____ television?

15. My roommate and I have decided _____ television.

16. I feel like _____ television.

17. They considered _____ television.

18. He keeps _____ television.

19. When you're tired, you seem _____ television.

20. Are they going to the movies or planning _____ television?

Use the correct form—gerund or infinitive—of the verbs in parentheses to complete this article. (Note: In some cases, both the gerund and the infinitive will be correct.)

TOO ANGRY ___to remember___ THE COMMERCIALS?
1. (remember)

According to a new study, _____ violent TV
2. (watch)

shows makes it difficult _____ brand names or
3. (recall)

commercial messages. Violence creates anger, and instead of

_____ the commercials, viewers are attempting
4. (hear)

_____ themselves down after violent scenes. The
5. (calm)

conclusion: _____ violent programs may not be appealing for advertisers
6. (sponsor)

because it may not be profitable for them.

This conclusion is good news for the parents, teachers, and lawmakers who have

objections to violence on television and are struggling _____ what children
7. (limit)

can watch. They had a small victory in the late 1990s, when lawmakers and the television

industry designed a TV-ratings system. Unfortunately, Congress did not ask parents

_____ in _____ the system, and the industry does not invite
8. (participate)   **9. (create)**

parents _____ shows before it assigns ratings. As a result, the system is not
10. (preview)

totally reliable, and parents are still guessing about the content of the shows their kids watch.

Why are parents objecting to _____ violence in television shows? The
11. (have)

numbers tell the story: A typical child will see 8,000 murders and 100,000 acts of violence

between the ages of 3 and 12! It's impossible _____ that this input won't
12. (believe)

affect young children. In fact, researchers have noted the following possible consequences

of _____ this much violence:
13. (view)

1. Children may become less sensitive to other people's suffering.

2. They may also become fearful of _____ with other people.
14. (interact)

3. They may be more likely _____ in a way that is harmful to others.
15. (behave)

Studies have shown that a majority of people want commercial TV _____
16. (produce)
more educational and informational programs. In addition, more than 75 percent prefer

_____ the number of hours of TV that children watch, and the American
17. (limit)
Academy of Pediatrics recommends _____ children _____ more
18. (not permit)   19. (watch)
than one to two hours per day.

It's hard _____ why the entertainment industry resists _____
20. (understand)   21. (make)
changes. Parents, teachers, and doctors are urging the industry _____ clearer
22. (develop)
ratings and _____ violence in children's shows. What's more, violent TV
23. (get rid of)
shows don't seem _____ companies an effective way _____ their
24. (offer)   25. (advertise)
products. Even artists in the television business feel that it's time _____ the
26. (decrease)
amount of violence in American TV shows and have warned industry executives

_____ _____ change.
27. (not continue)   28. (avoid)
The industry may choose _____ attention to the public, but it will not be
29. (not pay)
able to ignore the government. Lawmakers want _____ the way networks
30. (investigate)
market violent shows to teenagers. They are also asking the industry _____
31. (schedule)
violence-free hours, when no violent content is allowed. Hopefully, parents in the United

States will someday feel good about _____ the family TV.
32. (turn on)

EXERCISE 3: Gerund or Infinitive?

A TV talk-show host is talking to a doctor about children and TV violence. Complete the interview with the appropriate word or phrase from the boxes plus the gerund or infinitive form of the verb in parentheses.

fed up with	likely	~~shocked~~	unwilling	used to

HOST: I was _____*shocked to learn*_____ that children will see 100,000 acts of violence on
1. (learn)
television before they are 12. I had no idea it was that bad. It also appears that the networks

are _____. They seem pretty satisfied with things the way they are.
2. (change)

(continued on next page)

Doctor: Yes, I think that they're _____ all the responsibility on the viewer.
3. (put)
That's the way it's always been, and they're accustomed to it.

Host: The networks may not want to change, but I know a lot of us are really very

_____ violence during family viewing times. We're really sick of it.
4. (see)
A lot of my friends don't even turn on the cartoons anymore.

Doctor: That's probably a good idea. Several studies show that children are much more

_____ others after they watch violent cartoons. It's really
5. (hit)
quite predictable.

decide	dislike	force	hesitate	stop

Host: OK. Now what can we do about this problem?

Doctor: Well, viewers can make a big difference. First of all, we have to put a lot of pressure on the

networks and _____ them _____ shows
6. (rate)
more clearly. They'll give in if enough viewers tell them they must.

Host: What else?

Doctor: When you see something you don't like, pick up the phone immediately. Don't wait.

We shouldn't _____ the networks about material that we find
7. (tell)
offensive. Recently a network _____ a violent ad in some regions
8. (run)
of the country right in the middle of a family sitcom. So many people complained that they

reversed that decision and _____ the ad in that time slot.
9. (show)

Host: Violence bothers my kids, but they _____ a show once it starts.
10. (turn off)
They want to stick it out to the end.

consider	forbid	insist on	permit

Doctor: Parents have to assert their authority and _____ the channel when
11. (change)
violence appears. Sometimes they'll face a lot of resistance, but they should be firm.

Host: You know, in a lot of families, parents work until six. They can't successfully

_____ their children _____ certain
12. (turn on)
shows. They're just not around to enforce the rules.

DOCTOR: There's help from the electronics industry in the form of a V-chip.

HOST: What exactly is a V-chip?

DOCTOR: It's a chip built into television sets. The V-chip doesn't _____

children _____ to violent shows. It blocks them electronically.
 13. (tune in)

HOST: The V-chip and parental controls on satellite and cable TV are something all parents should

_____.
 14. (use)

| advise | agree | hesitate | keep |

HOST: All right. Is there anything else that you _____ parents

_____?
 15. (do)

DOCTOR: Parents must _____ with their children. They shouldn't
 16. (communicate)

_____ their kids about their feelings and opinions—and especially
 17. (ask)

about their activities.

HOST: Thank you, Doctor, for _____ to us today.
 18. (speak)

EXERCISE 4: Objects with Gerunds and Infinitives

Read the conversations about watching television. Then use the correct forms of the words in parentheses to write summaries.

1. **KIDS:** Can we watch TV now?

   MOM: I'm sorry, but you have to finish your homework first.

   SUMMARY: _____ *Their mother didn't allow them to watch TV.* _____
   (their mother / allow / they / watch TV)

2. **ANNIE:** My parents finally bought me a new TV, but it has a V-chip.

   BEA: What's that?

   ANNIE: It's something that blocks violent shows so that I can't watch them.

   SUMMARY: _____
   (a V-chip / interfere with / Annie / watch violent shows)

3. **ROGER:** Our kids really seem to like *Rappin' Reading*.

   CORA: I know. It's so great that there's high-quality TV about reading and learning.

   SUMMARY: _____
   (the show / encourage / they / get interested in books)

(continued on next page)

4. **DAD:** You were having some pretty bad nightmares last night, Jennifer. I think you'd

better stop watching those cop shows.

JENNIFER: OK, but I really love them.

SUMMARY: _____

(her father / tell / Jennifer / watch cop shows / anymore)

5. **STUDENT:** We want to watch the TV news, but the reporting on adult news shows is usually

really frightening.

TEACHER: Try *Youth Views*. It's a great news program for kids.

SUMMARY: _____

(the teacher / recommend / they / watch news for children)

6. **SUE:** I'll never forget that great Knicks game we watched last year.

BOB: What Knicks game?

SUE: Don't you remember? We saw it together! The Knicks beat the Rockets 91–85.

SUMMARY: _____

(Bob / remember / they / see that game)

7. **FRED:** Does Sharif still watch *Z-Men* every Saturday?

ABU: No. We explained that it was much too violent for him, and he decided not to

watch it anymore.

SUMMARY: _____

(Sharif's parents / persuade / he / watch the cartoon)

8. **MOM:** Sara, it's nine o'clock. Time to turn off the TV.

SARA: Oh, Mom. Just a little longer, OK?

MOM: You know the rules. No TV after nine o'clock.

SUMMARY: _____

(the mother / insist on / Sara / turn off the TV)

9. **AZIZA:** This is boring. What's on the other channels?

BEN: I don't know. Where's the remote control?

SUMMARY: _____

(Aziza / want / Ben / change the channel)

10. **PAUL:** *Primer Reportaje*, my favorite TV news program, starts in five minutes.

NICK: I've never understood why you watch that show. It's in Spanish, and you don't

speak Spanish at all.

SUMMARY: _____

(Nick / can't get used to / Paul / watch a Spanish-language news program)

Read the student's essay. There are eleven mistakes in the use of the gerund and infinitive. The first mistake is already corrected. Find and correct ten more.

Asoka Jayawardena
English 220
May 30

Violence on TV

            hearing
I'm tired of ~~hear~~ that violence on TV causes violence at home, in school, and on the streets. Almost all young people watch TV, but not all of them are involved in committing crimes! In fact, very few people choose acting in violent ways. To watch TV, therefore, is not the cause.

    Groups like the American Medical Society should stop making a point of to tell people what to watch. If we want living in a free society, it is necessary having freedom of choice. Children need learn values from their parents. It should be the parents' responsibility alone deciding what their child can or cannot watch. The government and other interest groups should avoid to interfere in these personal decisions. Limiting our freedom of choice is not the answer. If parents teach their children respecting life, children can enjoy to watch TV without any negative effects.

EXERCISE 6: Personal Writing

On a separate piece of paper, write a paragraph about a television show that you feel everyone, both adults and children, should watch. Use some of the phrases from the box.

I can't remember . . .	The show will allow . . .
I really like . . .	These days, it is not easy . . .
I recommend . . .	This is a wonderful show for anyone who wants . . .
In addition to . . .	Watching this show is . . .
The program is a great way . . .	Without a doubt, everyone will enjoy . . .

EXERCISE 1: Contrast: *Make, Have, Let, Help,* and *Get*

Complete the article about the roles that animals can play in our lives. Circle the correct verbs.

The Animal–Human Connection

Can pets get / (help) humans lead better lives? Not only animal lovers but also some
1.

health-care professionals believe that pets let / get us improve our quality of everyday living.
2.

Pets have / help their owners stay healthy. For example, dogs need daily exercise, and
3.

this has / makes many owners turn off their television sets or computers and go outside for
4.

a walk. While walking their dogs, they get the health rewards of being physically active,

and they are able to talk to the people they see on the street or in the park. These positive

human relationships get / make dog owners feel happy, which can lead to longer, healthier
5.

lives. Speaking of positive relationships, it is interesting to note that research shows pet

owners often have lower blood pressure as a result of spending time with their animals. It

seems that pets get / make their owners to relax.
6.

Animals can also play an important role for humans who are sick. In some cases,

health-care professionals let / get animals to provide
7.

attention, affection, and companionship for their patients.

The animals don't replace other forms of medical care,

but they help / have patients recover more quickly and live
8.

longer. The Delta Society is a nonprofit organization that

promotes the idea of using animals in places such as hospitals, nursing homes, and rehabilitation centers. The society <u>lets / gets</u> volunteers to work with those in need, but it
9.
doesn't <u>let / make</u> just any pet participate in its programs. It <u>makes / gets</u> pets and their
10.   11.
owners complete training courses so that the animals will be friendly and give comfort to the humans they meet.

In addition to helping those who are ill, animals can assist people with disabilities. Guide dogs <u>help / make</u> people who are blind cross busy streets or take public
12.
transportation. People who are unable to move their arms or legs can <u>help / have</u> their dogs
13.
open doors, turn lights off and on, and even answer the telephone. Special hearing dogs

<u>make / let</u> hearing-impaired owners pay attention when the doorbell rings, their baby cries,
14.
or a fire alarm sounds.

EXERCISE 2: *Make, Have, Get,* and *Help* + Object

Read the tip sheet from an animal welfare agency. Complete the sentences by adding pronoun objects and the correct form of the verbs in parentheses.

Dogs Are Family Members Too

Whether your family has a dog or you'd like to bring a dog into your home, here are some things to consider.

If you're thinking about getting a dog . . .

- It takes time and money to care for a dog. Be sure that you have enough of both. A dog could be a member of your family for 15 years or more.

- Talking to everyone in your family will make _____*them feel*_____ part of the
1. (feel)
decision-making process, and they'll be more likely to welcome a dog as a new member of the family.

- Pets are not always welcome. As one former pet owner says, find out if your landlord will let

_____ a dog in your apartment.
2. (keep)

(continued on next page)

- There are always animals available for adoption. Before buying a dog from a pet shop or a breeder, contact your local animal shelter. It's the humane thing to do. At the shelter, ask about classes or an adoption program that will help _____ what kind of dog is best for you and
  3. (decide)
  your family. Also talk to staff members about the health and history of a dog that you want to adopt. It's a good idea to have _____ you as much information as possible.
  4. (give)

If there are children in the family . . .

- Your child may really want a dog, and she may promise to take care of your family's new pet, but honestly, it may be impossible to get _____ it. Consider dividing pet-care
  5. (do)
  responsibilities among all members of the family, including children. It doesn't have to be complicated. Depending on the children's ages, it's certainly possible to have _____
  6. (take care of)
  specific tasks such as taking the dog for a walk after school or giving the dog food and water.

- Children may have to learn to be gentle. Get _____ animals need respect
  7. (realize)
  just like humans, and that means no hitting, kicking, riding, or pulling the tail of the family dog.

- At some point, your dog will get overexcited when he is playing. Children should know what to do to get
  _____.
  8. (calm down)

- It pays to be careful. If you have a very young child, she may love the family pet, but never let
  _____ with the family dog alone. Adult supervision is essential.
  9. (play)

If there is a new baby coming into the family . . .

- Your dog will know that there's been a change, and he will probably be excited, anxious, and quite curious. It's up to you to help _____. Before the baby arrives, introduce
  10. (adjust)
  him to baby sounds. He should also get accustomed to seeing a baby, so it's a good idea to use a doll or
  let _____ time around a real infant if possible.
  11. (spend)

- Your dog may need training so that you can get _____ you at all times
  12. (obey)
  when he is around the new baby. Remember to use positive rewards, not punishment.

- Although you'll be very busy with your new baby, spending some time with your dog will make
  _____ that he is still an important member of the family. It will also help
  13. (understand)
  _____ during this very exciting time in your life.
  14. (relax)

If you want to know more, contact our organization and let _____ you with
15. (provide)
more detailed information on dogs and families.

Read the conversations. Then use the correct forms of the verbs in parentheses to complete the summaries. Add pronouns when necessary.

1. **JOHN:** Mom, can I get a horse?

    MOTHER: No, of course you can't get a horse!

    SUMMARY: John's mother _____ *didn't let him get a horse.* _____
    (let)

2. **MOTHER:** Instead of a horse, will you agree to adopt a dog or a cat?

    JOHN: OK.

    SUMMARY: John's mother _____
    (get)

3. **MOTHER:** You can make the choice.

    JOHN: I'd rather have a cat.

    SUMMARY: His mother _____
    (let)

4. **MOTHER:** Now, you have to do some research on pet care.

    JOHN: I can do that. I know a couple of animal-protection groups that have good

    information on their websites.

    SUMMARY: She _____
    (make)

5. **JOHN:** Do I have to do all of the research by myself?

    MOTHER: Yes, you do.

    SUMMARY: John's mother _____
    (help)

6. **JOHN:** I found out that I have to be 18 to adopt a pet. Can you fill out and sign the adoption

    application forms for me?

    MOTHER: Sure.

    SUMMARY: John _____
    (get)

7. **MOTHER:** First, you have to explain the adoption process to me.

    JOHN: I have all of the information right here.

    SUMMARY: John's mother _____
    (have)

8. **JOHN:** I have enough money to pay the adoption fees.

    MOTHER: You may need the money later. I'll pay the fees.

    SUMMARY: John's mother _____
    (make)

EXERCISE 4: Editing

Read the university student's email. She made seven mistakes in the use of **make, have, let, help,** *and* **get.** *The first mistake is already corrected. Find and correct six more.*

Hi, Ami!

Thanks for staying in touch. Your emails always make me ~~to smile~~ *smile*—even when I'm feeling stressed. Knowing that I have a good friend like you really helps me relaxing and not take things so seriously.

At the end of last semester, my roommates and I decided to get a dog. Actually, my roommates made the decision and then got me go along with it. I made them promise to take care of the dog, but guess who's doing most of the work?! Don't misunderstand me. I love Ellie and appreciate what a great companion she is. I take her for a walk every morning and every night and make her run and play in the park near our apartment as often as I can because I know how much she enjoys it. Still, I wish I could have my roommates to spend just an hour a week with "our" dog. At this point, I can't even get them feeding Ellie, and now they want to move to an apartment complex that won't let us to have a dog. I think I'm going to have to choose whether to live with my roommates or with Ellie—and I think I'm going to choose Ellie!

Neha

EXERCISE 5: Personal Writing

On a separate piece of paper, write a paragraph about an experience with a pet. It can be your own experience, or one you've learned about from a friend, a TV show, or a movie. Use some of the phrases from the box.

I had to help . . .	Pets make me . . .
I was happy when I got the animal . . .	When it comes to pets, I would . . .
In my opinion, having a pet is . . .	You can always get . . .

UNIT 11 Phrasal Verbs: Review

EXERCISE 1: Particles

Complete the phrasal verbs with particles from the box. You will use some particles more than once.

ahead	down	on	over
back	off	out	up

Phrasal Verb	**Meaning**
1. catch ___on___	*become popular*
2. cheer _____	*make someone feel happier*
3. do _____	*do again*
4. get _____	*make progress, succeed*
5. let _____	*allow to leave*
6. let _____	*disappoint*
7. look _____	*examine*
8. pick _____	*select or identify*
9. take _____	*return*
10. try _____	*use to find out if it works*
11. turn _____	*raise the volume*
12. turn _____	*lower the volume*
13. use _____	*consume*
14. write _____	*write on a piece of paper*
15. put _____	*delay*
16. think _____	*invent*

EXERCISE 2: Phrasal Verbs

Read about New Year traditions around the world. Complete the article with the correct forms of the phrasal verbs from the box. Choose the verbs that are closest in meaning to the words in parentheses.

burn up	get together	go back	~~pay back~~	put together	throw away
cut down	give out	go out	put on	set up	

Starting New

Wearing new clothes, _____*paying back*_____
1. (repay)
debts, lighting candles—many cultures share similar

New Year traditions. In Iran, for example, people

celebrate *Now Ruz*, or New Day, on the first day of

spring. A few days before the festival, families _____ bushes and
2. (bring down by cutting)

_____ piles of wood. They set the piles on fire, and before the wood
3. (assemble)

_____ , each family member jumps over one of the fires and says, "I
4. (burn completely)

give you my pale face, and I take your red one." The day before the New Year begins, the

family _____ a table in the main room with special foods and
5. (prepare for use)

objects, such as colored eggs, cake, and the *haft-sin*, seven objects with names beginning

with the sound "s." Everyone _____ new clothes, and the family
6. (cover the body with)

_____ around the table. When the New Year begins, family members
7. (meet)

hug each other and _____ gifts, especially to the children. It all
8. (distribute)

makes for a very festive environment. For the next 12 days, people visit each other, but on

the thirteenth day, it is unlucky to be inside a house, so people _____
9. (leave)

and spend the day in parks and fields, where they have picnics, listen to music, and play

sports. They don't _____ home until sunset. At the end of the day,
10. (return)

everyone "_____" bad luck by throwing wheat or lentils into a river.
11. (discard)

EXERCISE 3: Phrasal Verbs and Objects

Complete the conversations with the phrasal verbs and objects in parentheses. Place the object between the verb and the participle when possible.

A.   **Vijay:** We need about two dozen candles for Diwali.

    Nira: I'll _____*pick them up*_____ after work.
        1. (pick up / them)

    Vijay: While you're there, why don't you get some new decorations?

    Nira: Let's have the children _____. You know how
               2. (pick out / them)

    excited they get about the Hindu New Year.

B.   **Eva:** Why do you _____ on Rosh Hashana?
        1. (empty out / the money and everything else in your pockets)

    Simon: It's a custom for the Jewish New Year to throw what's in our pockets into moving water.

    It's like getting rid of last year's bad memories.

    Eva: Cigarettes are harmful. Here's my lighter. Let's _____.
                                2. (throw away / it)

C.   **May:** When will we _____ for the Chinese New Year?
               1. (set off / the firecrackers)

    Ning: Not until dark.

    May: Don't the firecrackers have something to do with evil spirits?

    Ning: Yes. We believe that the noise _____.
                         2. (keep away / them)

D.   **Liam:** Are you decorating for Christmas?

    Zoé: No, we're _____ for Kwanzaa, the
             1. (hang up / these streamers)

    African-American harvest celebration. It comes at the same time as Christmas and

    New Year's Day.

    Liam: What is your mom putting on the table?

    Zoé: A *kinara*. We _____ to hold the Kwanzaa candles.
                  2. (set up / it)

E. **Kelsey:** Do you usually make New Year's resolutions?

    Ian: Yes, and I _____ because they're so easy to
       1. (write down / all of the resolutions that I make each year)
    forget by February.

    Kelsey: I need to do more than that. This year I'm going to hire a food consultant. My resolution

    is to stop eating desserts.

    Ian: I _____ for a few months last year. I lost more
            2. (gave up / them)
    than five pounds.

Read the list of New Year's resolutions. There are eleven mistakes in the use of phrasal verbs. The first mistake is already corrected. Find and correct ten more.

<u>New Year's Resolutions</u>

Wake ~~out~~ ^{up} earlier. (No later than 7:30!)

Work out at the gym at least 3 times a week.

Lose 5 pounds. (Give over eating so many desserts.)

Be more conscious of the environment:

— Don't throw down newspapers. Recycle them.

— Save energy. Turn on the lights and TV when I leave the apartment.

Straighten up my room and make it more comfortable:

— Hang out my clothes when I take off them.

— Put my books back where they belong.

— Give some of my old books and clothing that I no longer wear away.

— Read about feng shui theory to increase positive energy.

Don't put off doing my math homework even when the problems seem complex. Finish the assignments, and hand in them on time!

Read more.

Use the dictionary more. (Look over words I don't know.)

When someone calls and leaves a message, call them back right away. Don't put off it!

Get to know my neighbors. Ask them for coffee over.

Write a paragraph about how people celebrate birthdays in your home country. Use some of the phrases from the box.

In many countries, the person who is celebrating a birthday blows out . . .

In my home country, birthdays are . . .

Instead of birthdays, we celebrate . . .

On my birthday, I always think about . . .

People in my country usually dress up / don't dress up . . .

The most interesting thing about birthday celebrations in . . .

We sometimes get together with . . .

When we get through with . . .

EXERCISE 1: Particles

Complete the phrasal verbs with the correct particles.

Phrasal Verb	Meaning
1. call ___back___	return a phone call
2. get _____	recover from an illness or a bad situation
3. cross _____	draw a line through
4. call _____	cancel
5. drop _____	visit unexpectedly
6. look _____	be careful
7. keep _____	continue
8. talk _____	persuade
9. blow _____	explode
10. turn _____	reject
11. run _____	meet accidentally
12. put _____	return to its original place
13. work _____	solve
14. go _____	continue
15. find _____	discover
16. turn _____	lower the volume

Complete the paragraphs with the appropriate form of the phrasal verbs from the boxes.

catch on	figure out	help out	team up with	turn on
~~come out~~	go off	take away	turn off	

A. There have been a lot of changes since the first consumer

cell phones _____*came out*_____ in the 1980s.
1.

The original phones were big, heavy, and very expensive.

After designers _____ how to
2.

make them smaller and more affordable, they really began

to _____. Now, people all over
3.

the world are _____ their mobile
4.

phones and using them in ways that could never have

been imagined in the 1980s. Several years ago, wireless

companies _____ digital-photography experts to produce camera
5.

phones, which are now popular with consumers. Internet access is another way that cell

phones _____ us _____ by keeping us
6.

connected and informed. Today, smart phones are almost the equivalent of a small computer.

However, there is a negative side to wireless technology. For example, when cell phones

constantly _____ in restaurants, movie theaters, and classrooms,
7.

they can be annoying. When we're forced to listen to other people's conversations in public

places, it _____ our privacy and the privacy of the person talking
8.

on the phone. Clearly, it's sometimes best to _____ our cell phones

_____.
9.

(continued on next page)

| end up | keep up with | pick out | use up |
| find out | look over | put away | watch out for |

B. Cell phones let us _____ 1. friends and family whenever and wherever

we want, but they can _____ 2. being very expensive. It's great to stay

in touch, but it's hard to know when to stop talking and _____ our

mobile phones _____ 3. . Cell phone companies advertise reasonably

priced calling packages, but it's easy to _____ 4. all the minutes on a basic

plan. Many of us have _____ 5. the hard way what it's like to pay overage

charges. Smart consumers do comparison shopping and _____ 6. wireless

service with features such as free weekend and evening minutes, unlimited calls to individual

family members, and no roaming charges when customers go out of their calling area. Smart

consumers also _____ 7. their cell phone contract carefully before they

sign it. They realize how important it is to _____ 8. hidden fees.

EXERCISE 3: Phrasal Verbs and Object Pronouns

Complete the conversations. Use phrasal verbs and pronouns.

1. **Luis:** I thought you were going to ask the Riveras over for dinner.

   Ines: I did. I ____ *asked them over* ____ for Friday night.

2. **Luis:** Did you invite their son too? He gets along well with Jimmy.

   Ines: That's a good idea. He really does _____.

3. **Ines:** If you run into Marta tomorrow, invite her too. She knows the Riveras.

   Luis: I usually don't _____ on Tuesdays. If we want her to come,

   we should call.

4. **Ines:** I'd like you to straighten up your room before the Riveras come over.

   Jimmy: No problem. I'll _____ right after school on Friday.

5. **Jimmy:** There's a big game on TV at eight o'clock on Friday that I'd like to watch. Do we really

   have to get together with the Riveras then?

   Ines: Yes, we do. We haven't _____ since last summer. Besides, we

   canceled our dinner plans last month, and I don't want to cancel again.

6. INES: Maybe you could pick out some CDs to play during dinner.

    JIMMY: Sure. I'll _____ right now.

7. INES: I hope we can count on the Riveras to bring the dessert.

    LUIS: Don't worry. You can _____. If they promised to bring

    dessert, then they'll bring it.

8. INES: You can bring out the roast now. It's done.

    LUIS: Great. I'll _____ right away so we can eat. It smells great.

9. INES: Be careful! Don't pick up the pan without pot holders! It's hot!

    LUIS: Ow! Too late! I just _____.

10. LUIS: I'm going to turn down the music. It's a little too loud.

    INES: Oh, don't get up. I'll _____.

11. LUIS: Should I cover up the leftovers?

    INES: Uh-huh. Here's some aluminum foil. After you _____, you

    can put them in the refrigerator.

12. INES: You didn't eat much at dinner tonight. You're really sticking to your diet, aren't you?

    LUIS: That's right. I've _____ for three weeks now, and I plan to

    continue until I lose 15 pounds.

13. INES: Could you help me put away these folding chairs?

    LUIS: Why don't you rest? I'll _____.

14. INES: Don't forget to turn on the dishwasher before you go to bed.

    LUIS: I'll _____ now. That way I won't forget.

15. INES: We got a phone call during dinner, but I can't identify this number on the caller ID. I

    wish I could figure out who called.

    LUIS: It's late, and I'm tired. Let's go to sleep. We can _____

    tomorrow morning.

See if you can figure out the puzzle.

Across

4. Gets off (the bus)
7. Want
11. Mix up
13. Figure out
16. Opposite of *fall*
17. Leave out
18. Think up
19. These can run out of ink.
21. _____ it rains, it pours.
23. Call up
25. Don't go away. Please _____.
26. Street (*abbreviation*)
27. Middle
31. Call off
32. Indefinite article
33. Professional (*short form*)
34. Medical doctor (*abbreviation*)
36. What time _____ she usually show up?
38. Negative word
40. Take place
41. Put up (a building)

Down

1. Pick _____ up at 5:00. I'll be ready then.
2. Hello
3. You and I
4. Pick up
5. Advertisements (*short form*)
6. Hands in
7. Talk over
8. Tell off
9. Take back
10. Carry on
12. Look over
14. *am, is,* _____
15. Eastern Standard Time (*abbreviation*)
18. Drop _____ on
19. Put off
20. Come in
21. The music is loud. Please turn _____ down.
22. Pass out
24. Blow up
27. Her book _____ out last year.
28. Marcia always _____ up with more work than anyone else.
29. Rte. (*full word*)
30. *Drop in* means "to _____ unexpectedly."
31. You put a small bandage on it.
35. Don't guess. Look it _____.
37. Please go _____. Don't stop.
39. Either . . . _____

Read the opinion piece that Luis is planning to send to his local newspaper. There are eight mistakes in the use of phrasal verbs. The first mistake is already corrected. Find and correct seven more.

In my opinion, drivers should hang ~~on~~ *up* their phones and turn off them the minute they get in their cars. This is the best way to eliminate some of the careless accidents on the streets of our city. After all, is it more important to keep up your friends and business associates with or save lives and money? I have looked into this matter and found some alarming statistics on mobile phones and accidents out. Research from the National Safety Council points out that cell phones and texting cause 1.6 million accidents each year. Clearly, it's time for drivers to get in the phone. And it's time for lawmakers to come over with a plan to make all phone use by motorists illegal, including the use of headsets and other hands-free technology. They must create a law to turn into our streets safe places for drivers and pedestrians alike. Then the local authorities must carry out it.

EXERCISE 6: Personal Writing

On a separate piece of paper, write a paragraph about the ways that you use a cell phone. Use some of the phrases from the box.

I really count on . . .	I'm afraid to miss out on . . . , so . . .
I think that I should look into . . .	Like most people, I would like to cut down on . . .
I usually turn my phone off when . . .	One of these days, I'm going to end up . . .
I'll never give up . . .	When my friends call me up, . . .

UNIT 13   Adjective Clauses with Subject Relative Pronouns

EXERCISE 1: Placement of Adjective Clauses

Put each adjective clause directly after the noun that it describes. Draw an arrow to show the correct placement.

1. People look at the brighter side of life.

   that have an optimistic personality

2. Some people assume we are born with personality traits.

   which control all our feelings and actions

3. Researchers contradict that idea.

   whose work is in the field of positive psychology

4. Positive psychologists offer practical advice for anyone.

   who wants a better chance of being happy

5. One activity is making a list of three good things in your life.

   that helps to improve feelings of happiness

6. Having a close friend also increases the possibility of happiness.

   who cares about you

7. Interestingly, a mother doesn't seem to be any happier than a woman with no children.

   whose children are grown

Meghana is doing a research assignment about happiness. Read her notes. Circle the correct relative pronouns.

— The dictionary defines happiness as a feeling (that) / who comes from a
  1.
pleasurable or satisfying experience. A person who / whose life is happy
  2.
doesn't need to be a millionaire. The things that / who make us happy often
  3.
have nothing to do with money or luxury.

— A woman who / whose wins the lottery might be happy, but not for long.
  4.
Stories who / which appear in newspapers and magazines point out how
  5.
quickly the money disappears and how lottery winners often end up looking

for something that / who will bring them more contentment.
  6.

— To achieve happiness, a job who / which is challenging or an experience
  7.
that / who allows people to grow and learn is better than money. Is it the
  8.
feeling of accomplishment that / who leads to happiness?
  9.

— Research shows the importance of genetics. About 50 percent of the

differences who / which exist between a man who / whose says he is happy
  10.   **11.**
and one that / which claims to be unhappy are a result of birth.

— Martin Seligman, that / who directs the Positive Psychology Center at the
  13.
University of Pennsylvania, says happiness requires effort. Seligman has

clients and students who / whose feelings have changed dramatically with
  14.
happiness training.

— Personal relationships are clearly important, but there's still a question

that / who bothers me. If people who / whose romantic relationships are
  15.   **16.**
strong feel happy, why are there so many divorces?

— Remember to look at the Journal of Personality and Social Psychology,

that / which will certainly have useful articles. Check for other information
  17.
that / who is in the online database at the library.
  18.

Read the article about how to stay a happy couple. Complete it with a relative pronoun and the correct forms of the verbs in parentheses.

Congratulations! You've finally found Ms. or Mr. Right. You're now a couple—two people _____*who*_____ _____*love*_____ each

1. (love)

other's company, _____ at each

2. (laugh)

other's jokes, and _____ to be

3. (plan)

together forever. Of course, you both want to make this a relationship _____

_____ feeling wonderful. But how? Read this advice from several couples

4. (keep)

_____ marriages _____ to be successful after many years.

5. (continue)

Respect your partner's personality type. Opposites attract, but they also require a lot

of understanding. Heidi, _____ _____ an extreme introvert, fell

6. (be)

in love with her partner Dave partly because of his warm personality, _____

still always _____ her feel very special. And Dave, _____

7. (make)

_____ Heidi's need for a lot of time time alone, gets similar respect from Heidi,

8. (respect)

_____ _____ his going to some social events without her.

9. (not mind)

Feel lucky. Sometimes luck is a question of attitude. Those couples _____

_____ that they are lucky to have each other are the ones _____

10. (feel)

_____ good luck in everyday events. They don't wait to win the lottery. They

11. (find)

see luck in their partner's little successes and in their own happiness.

Write your own history. Think of your marriage as a wonderful story _____

_____ a reality and history of its own. Family stories and photographs are the

12. (have)

tools _____ _____ this reality back to life during the bad times.

13. (bring)

Believe in each other. Trust is even more important than love, _____

_____ and _____ during a long marriage. This is the feeling

14. (increase)   **15. (decrease)**

_____ _____ each partner feel safe in the relationship. It's also the

16. (make)

condition _____ _____ people grow and change as they must.
17. (help)

Spend time together. It's not so easy in today's world, but if you want a relationship

_____ _____ , it's what you need. Develop the ability to simply
18. (last)

enjoy being together. Couples _____ _____ this don't even have
19. (do)

to talk to feel close. Remember, your relationship, _____ _____
20. (feel)

so perfect right now, is going to change over time. These five suggestions from successful

couples can help you appreciate the good times and survive the difficult ones.

EXERCISE 4: Sentence Combining

Combine the pairs of sentences. Make the second sentence in each pair an adjective clause.
Make any other necessary changes.

1. I met Rebecca in 1994. Rebecca is now my wife.

   I met Rebecca, who is now my wife, in 1994.

2. She was visiting her favorite aunt. Her aunt's apartment was right across from mine.

   _____

3. I was immediately attracted to Rebecca because of her unique smile. The smile was full of
   warmth and good humor.

   _____

4. I could see that Rebecca had a fun-loving personality. Her interests were similar to mine.

   _____

5. Ballroom dancing was one of our favorite activities. Ballroom dancing was very popular in
   those days.

   _____

6. We also enjoyed playing cards with some of our close friends. Our friends lived in the
   neighborhood.

   _____

7. Our friend Mike taught us how to ski. Mike was a professional skier.

   _____

8. We got married in a ski lodge. The ski lodge was in Vermont.

   _____

(continued on next page)

9. Our marriage has grown through the years. Our marriage means a lot to us both.

_____

10. The love and companionship have gotten stronger. The love and companionship make us very happy.

_____

11. Even the bad things have brought us closer together. Bad things have happened.

_____

12. I really love Rebecca. Rebecca makes me feel truly happy.

_____

EXERCISE 5: Editing

Read Meghana's paragraph about how psychologists measure happiness. There are ten mistakes in the use of adjective clauses. The first mistake is already corrected. Find and correct nine more.

                         focuses

Psychological research that ~~focus~~ on happiness requires a tool that can measure a person's feelings. A number of well-known researchers who they collect this type of data claim to have a simple method that work well. They ask just one question, which is "How happy are you?" People which respond to the question usually give their answer with a number. For example, on a scale of 1–10, a 1 would be "extremely unhappy" and a 10 would be "extremely happy." Professor Ed Diener, that is a leading U.S. psychologist, says the method is surprisingly effective because it produces answers that is honest and real. Of course there may be someone who feelings change throughout the day, so there is a related type of measurement who uses handheld computers to send messages to research participants to find out what they are doing at different times and what their mood is. Technology is also important for scientists which make a connection between happiness and the human body. When they see a person whose skin temperature have risen, they know the person is happy. This group of researchers believes their method of measuring happiness through body heat, blood pressure, heart rate, and brain waves is quite effective.

EXERCISE 6: Personal Writing

Circle the best number to show your level of happiness.

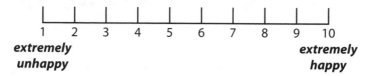

Write a paragraph to explain your answer. Use some of the phrases from the box.

I am the kind of person who . . .	The thing that makes . . .
In my opinion, happy people are those . . .	The word that describes . . .
My favorite / least favorite activity, which . . .	There are people in my life whose . . .
The most important . . .	

UNIT 14 Adjective Clauses with Object Relative Pronouns or *When* and *Where*

EXERCISE 1: Relative Pronouns and *When* and *Where*: Subject and Object

Circle the correct words to complete the book acknowledgments and dedications.

I couldn't have written this memoir without the lessons <u>what /(that)</u> I learned from my parents.
1.

With them, I found my place in a new world, while never losing my connections to the world

<u>that / who</u> we left behind. The courage and creativity with <u>which / that</u> they faced a new life and
2.   **3.**

culture have made it possible for me to write about our journey.

(Irina Pawlak, *Finding Your Place: A Memoir of Discovery*. Chicago, Hemerion Press, 2011.)

These stories, <u>that / which</u> I wrote over a period of ten years, are dedicated to my students at the
4.

Branton College Writing Program. The excitement <u>whose / that</u> they bring to the job of turning life
5.

into literature continues to inspire my own writing. The issues <u>which / who</u> we all face never
6.

change, but there has not been a day <u>where / when</u> a student hasn't taught me a new way to
7.

look at one of those issues. It's a debt <u>that / whom</u> is impossible for me to repay.
8.

(Patrick O'Doyle, *Fixed in Our Ways: Short Stories*. Atlanta, Sandbar Press, 2010.)

This book, <u>which / who</u> you are holding in your hands, would not have been possible without the help
9.

of many people. First of all, I'd like to thank everyone <u>that / which</u> I have ever met, for our lives are
10.

all shaped by our countless everyday encounters. Most of all, however, I want to thank the people

<u>which / who</u> I know best—my family and friends, without <u>whose / whom</u> you would not be reading
11.   **12.**

about all the people <u>whose / that</u> names I never even learned. I'd also like to express gratitude to my
13.

office desk, <u>when / where</u> I spent most of the last two years writing, and to my office chair, without
14.

<u>which / whose</u> strong support I am sure I would have suffered many a backache. Finally, I need to
15.

thank myself for any mistakes <u>that / where</u> you find in these pages. They are mine and mine alone.
16.

(Wolfgang Fremder, *Strangers and Other Friends*, Los Angeles, Knollcrest Books, 2008.)

I'd like to dedicate this book to Jean Auel, <u>which / whose</u> novel *The Clan of the Cave Bear* I read as

17.

a twelve-year-old. Lost in her story, I knew immediately that I wanted to study archeology. I hope

the young adults for <u>whom / who</u> I wrote this book will find the subject as fascinating as I did.

18.

Among all the people <u>that / where</u> I must thank, first is photographer Eli Garcia-Ramirez, on

19.

<u>whom / whose</u> photographs I based my earliest studies. At Altamira, <u>that / where</u> I first saw cave

20.   21.

paintings up close, I met other researchers in <u>whose / who</u> warm welcome I found the courage to

22.

keep on working. In 2009, <u>where / when</u> the book was as good as I could make it, my luck

23.

continued in my editor Jack Poulson, from <u>which / whom</u> I learned how to make it even better.

24.

(Melissa Cho, *Rock On! Stone Age Cave Paintings in Altamira*. Toronto, Breadlow Press, 2010.)

EXERCISE 2: Adjective Clauses with Relative Pronouns or *When* and *Where*

*Read the article about book dedications and acknowledgments. Complete the information with **who(m), which, that, whose, when,** or **where,** and the correct forms of the verbs in parentheses.*

To L. F., without _____<u>whose</u>_____ encouragement . . .

1.

Dedication and acknowledgement pages are the places _____ _____ an author

2.

_____ the people _____ support and assistance he or she

3. (thank)   4.

_____ valuable while writing. These words of gratitude are an issue because

5. (find)

they are probably the last ones _____ the author _____

6.   7. (write)

for a book, but they'll most likely be the first ones _____ other people

8.

_____. This fact may explain some of the problems _____

9. (read)   10.

writers _____ when preparing these pages. The thanks should be gracious

11. (face)

and well written, but the task of writing them most often comes at the end of a long

project—a time _____ an author sometimes _____ words.

12.   13. (run out of)

In the 16th and 17th centuries, _____ rich nobles _____

14.   15. (support)

artists, writers were often paid well for writing dedications in _____ they

16.

_____ their wealthy employers. Some "authors" avoided poverty by making

17. (praise)

a profession of dedication writing. They traveled the countryside carrying fake books into

(continued on next page)

_____ they _____ a new dedication: when each rich
   18.   **19. (insert)**
family invited them to stay at their home.

 The current generation of writers usually dedicates a book to a family member, friend, or

colleague with _____ he or she _____ deeply connected.
       20.   **21. (feel)**
The dedication page is short and often contains only the initials of the person or persons to

_____ the author _____ the work. However, in the
  22.   **23. (dedicate)**
acknowledgements, _____ the author _____ more room,
       24.   **25. (have)**
everyone from reference librarians to proofreaders is thanked.

 Unfortunately, most writers' handbooks give authors very little help with dedications and

acknowledgments. "It's just something _____ you _____
         26.   **27. (be supposed to)**
know how to handle," complains one author.

EXERCISE 3: Adjective Clauses with Relative Pronouns or *When* and *Where*

Combine the pairs of sentences, using **who(m), which, that, whose, when,** *or* **where.** *Make the second sentence in each pair an adjective clause. Make any other necessary changes.*

1. Jean M. Auel wrote a novel. I enjoyed reading it.

   Jean M. Auel wrote a novel which I enjoyed reading. _____

2. *The Clan of the Cave Bear* tells the story of a clan of prehistoric people. Auel started researching the book in 1977.

   _____

3. It took a lot of work to learn about these prehistoric people. Auel wanted to understand the prehistoric people's lives.

   _____

4. The clan lived during the Ice Age. Glaciers covered large parts of the Earth then.

   _____

5. The people lived near the shores of the Black Sea. There are a lot of large caves there.

   _____

6. The clan made their home in a large cave. Bears had lived in the cave.

   _____

7. The task of hunting had great importance in the life of the Cave Bear Clan. The men were responsible for the task of hunting.

   _____

8. One aspect of their lives was their technical skill. Auel describes that aspect well.

   _____

9. She learned some of the arts. Prehistoric people had practiced them.

   _____

10. In her preface, Auel thanks a man. She studied the art of making stone tools with him.

    _____

11. She also thanks an Arctic survival expert. She met him while she was doing research.

    _____

12. He taught her to make a snow cave on Mt. Hood. She spent one January night there.

    _____

13. She went through a difficult time. She couldn't write then.

    _____

14. A fiction writer inspired her to finish her book. She attended the writer's lecture.

    _____

15. Jean Auel's novel remains popular in translations around the world. She published the novel in 1980.

    _____

EXERCISE 4: Optional Deletions of Relative Pronouns

In five of the sentences in Exercise 3, the relative pronoun can be deleted. Rewrite the sentences below with the relative pronoun deleted.

1. _Jean M. Auel wrote a novel I enjoyed reading._

2. _____

3. _____

4. _____

5. _____

Read the student's book report. There are nine mistakes in the use of adjective clauses. The first mistake is already corrected. Find and correct eight more.

Jorge Ramos

English 220

For my book report, I read *The Clan of the Cave Bear*, ~~that~~ *which* Jean M. Auel wrote after several years of research. In this novel about the life of prehistoric people, the main character is Ayla. She is found by a wandering clan after an earthquake kills her family. The same earthquake destroyed the cave in which this clan had lived, and they are searching for another home. The clan leader wants to leave Ayla to die. She is an Other—a human which language and culture his clan doesn't understand. However, the leader's sister Iza, Ayla soon calls Mother, adopts her.

The story takes place at a time where human beings are still evolving. Ayla is a new kind of human. Her brain, which she can use it to predict and make plans, is different from Iza's and other clan members'. Their brains are adapted to memory, not new learning, whom they fear and distrust. At first, Ayla brings luck to the clan. She accidentally wanders into a place where they find a large cave, perfect for their new home. She is educated by Iza, who's great knowledge everyone respects. The skills that Iza passes on to Ayla include healing and magic, as well as finding food, cooking, and sewing. However, Ayla's powers make it impossible for her to stay with the clan. She learns to hunt, a skill where women are forbidden to practice. Her uncle, that she loves very much, allows her to stay with the clan, but after he dies, she loses his protection. Another earthquake, for which she is blamed, destroys the clan's home, and she is forced to leave.

EXERCISE 6: Personal Writing

Write a report about an excellent book that you've read. Use some of the phrases from the box.

One character whose personality I . . .	The main reason that . . .
The book which . . .	The place where . . .
The ending of the book, which you . . .	The time period when . . .
The final thing I . . .	This is a book everyone . . .

PART VII

MODALS: REVIEW AND EXPANSION

UNIT 15 Modals and Similar Expressions: Review

EXERCISE 1: Modals: Function

What is the meaning of the underlined modals and similar expressions? Choose from the functions in the box.

ability	assumption	necessity
advice	future possibility	prohibition

1. Anyone with family and friends in faraway places <u>ought to</u> use Skype to stay in touch.   *advice*

2. Skype is another way that we <u>can</u> stay connected online.   _____

3. You <u>must</u> register, but the calls cost nothing.   _____

4. That <u>can't</u> be right. There's no way Skype offers free service.   _____

5. That's true. Skype users <u>have got to</u> pay for calls to home and mobile phones, but Skype-to-Skype calls are free.   _____

6. I <u>couldn't</u> get online yesterday. My DSL wasn't working.   _____

7. You<u>'d better</u> find another Internet provider.   _____

8. <u>Should</u> I sign up for Skype on my smart phone?   _____

9. That type of service <u>might not</u> be free until sometime next year. Check the Skype website to find out.   _____

10. Skype has millions of fans worldwide. It <u>must</u> be easy to use.   _____

11. <u>Do</u> Skype users <u>have to</u> keep a regular phone for any reason?   _____

12. In the U.S., Skype <u>can't</u> provide calls to emergency numbers like 911 because U.S. laws don't allow it.   _____

13. You <u>should</u> always keep your Skype password secure.   _____

14. Skype accounts are private, so you <u>must not</u> log on with another user's name or password.   _____

15. I <u>may</u> call my parents on Skype later today.   _____

EXERCISE 2: Affirmative and Negative Statements

Complete the article with the correct affirmative or negative form of the verbs in parentheses.

Digital Know-How

Protect Yourself
by Karun Johnson   August 10, 2011

Even Mark Zuckerberg _____ had to have _____ one before he created his own Facebook
                                1. (have to / have)

page. Bill Gates _____ without one either. And now that you're involved in
                        2. (could / live)

social networking and shopping online, you need it too. After all, it's probably the number one way that you

_____ yourself. You _____ by now that I'm
            3. (can / protect)   4. (must / know)

talking about having a strong password for your online accounts.

This article is for all of you out there who still have passwords like "password" or "12345." I understand.

You're afraid that you _____ something more complicated. However, an
                        5. (may / remember)

effective password _____ a difficult one. In fact, you _____
                        6. (have to / be)   7. (should / choose)

something that you _____ easily. Start with a word or group of words that's
                        8. (be able to / recall)

meaningful to you, but not personal information like the name of your hometown, a family member, or a pet.

These are details that thieves _____ about you online and the first thing they'll
                        9. (might / find out)

use when they try to steal your password. Instead, you _____ of something
                        10. (ought to / think)

like the car you've always wanted, and begin with "red sports my dream." Then keep on going. To be safe, you

_____ the advice of the experts and add capital letters, numbers, and symbols.
        11. (had better / follow)

In the end, you _____ a great combination like **Ed$mydr#1** as your password.
                    12. (could / have)

You're feeling safer already, aren't you? But hold on! There are just a few more things that you

_____. Make a different password for each of your online accounts, and
        13. (have got to / do)

change them regularly. Most importantly, you _____ the passwords to anyone
                                                14. (must / give)

if you want to truly protect the personal content of your accounts.

Comments: 35

EXERCISE 3: Modals: Meaning

Read the conversations between two people who are going to a computer store. Circle the correct words to complete the conversations.

1. **A:** The computer store (might) / can't be crowded. It's Saturday.

   B: You're right. We 'd better / 'd better not leave right away.

2. **A:** Should / Might we take the subway?

   B: No. Let's drive. I'm not sure if I'll find what I'm looking for, but who knows? I must / might buy a new computer today. If I get one, I may not / can't bring it home on the subway.

3. **A:** I have to / don't have to be home by 5:00. I'm meeting my mother for dinner tonight.

   B: It's still early. We must not / can get back by 3:00.

4. **A:** Do you think it's going to rain?

   B: It may / may not. I don't see any clouds.

5. **A:** Hey, the sign says that you must not / don't have to park here. It's a loading area.

   B: Oh, I might not / couldn't see the sign. That bus was in the way.

6. **A:** Wow! Look at all these people in the store. There must / can be a sale today.

   B: Maybe we shouldn't / ought to come back another day.

   A: How can / should you say that? Let's see what's going on.

7. **A:** We 'd better not / might not wait to talk to a salesperson.

   B: You're right. Let's find someone now. Last week, I can't / wasn't able to get anyone in the store to help me. It's a good thing they have such low prices.

8. **A:** You may / ought to ask the salesperson if there's a discount for students.

   B: That's a good idea. I'll show him my student ID card. It mustn't / couldn't hurt.

9. **A:** You need a computer with a webcam. Otherwise, how can you / do you have to do video chats on Skype?

   B: You're right.

   A: How about this computer? It might / must be perfect for you.

10. **A:** Wow! The computer is only $200. That has to / couldn't be the right price. It's way too low.

    B: $200 is the amount you'll save off the regular price of the computer, but you may / must buy it today to get the savings.

11. **A:** I <u>couldn't / can't</u> believe what time it is! I'm going to be late for dinner with my mother.

    B: Don't worry. You'll still be home by 5:00, but we <u>'ve got to / 'd better not</u> leave right now.

12. **A:** Oh, no. My cell phone is ringing.

    B: Who <u>could / should</u> that be?

    A: It <u>must / couldn't</u> be my mother. She always calls when I'm late.

EXERCISE 4: Editing

Read the comment from Karun Johnson's blog. There are eight mistakes in the use of modals. The first mistake is already corrected. Find and correct seven more.

---

35 Comments
MaryE on August 11, 2011 at 3:00 PM,

I must ~~to say~~ *say* that Karun is absolutely correct about good passwords. You could not think they're important, but I'm here to tell you that you had better not pay attention to your online security. I had a major problem last year. I didn't able to use my credit card when I went shopping one day because someone had charged five or six big-screen TVs and airline tickets to my account and I had no more available credit. I couldn't believe it was happening to me. I must spend almost two months taking care of the problem, but I finally did. And I learned that this problem can happened to anyone, so we don't have to protect ourselves. I no longer have a "12345" password and you shouldn't use one either. May you think of a better way to protect your privacy—and your money?

EXERCISE 5: Personal Writing

On a separate piece of paper, write one paragraph giving your opinion about the best ways for students to use the Internet safely. Use some of the phrases from the box.

As a general rule, . . .	The first step that everyone should . . .
I was able to . . .	To protect themselves on the Internet, students must . . .
It might . . .	You don't have to . . .
Of course you can . . . , but . . .	You should never . . .

EXERCISE 1: Questions and Responses: Affirmative and Negative Statements

Complete the article with the correct form of the verbs in parentheses or with short answers. Choose between affirmative and negative forms.

I _Shouldn't Have Said_ **That!**
1. (should / say)
(Or, How to Stop Fighting Losing Battles)

All families argue, but when you've just had the same argument for the tenth or hundredth time, it's time to stop and think. Why did it happen again? What _____ you

_____ this time to make things different? For this week's column, we asked
2. (could / do)

Dr. Iva Gripe to answer some questions that readers frequently ask. Dr. Gripe works in the

field of clinical psychology and is an expert in resolving family conflicts.

Q: My husband promised to help around the house more. A week after his promise, his stuff was all

over the living room again. I pointed it out, and we had an argument. _____ I

_____ it pass and not said anything?
3. (should / let)

A: _____. You were probably a bit unrealistic. True change is a process
4.

that takes time. After just a week, you _____ him a break. I suggest
5. (could / give)

waiting 30 days before bringing up the subject again.

Q: My wife just bought a very expensive camera. I felt she _____ it with
6. (might / discuss)

me first, but I didn't want to start a fight. Instead, I decided not to buy some clothes I need. I don't

feel comfortable with that decision. How _____ I _____ this
7. (should / handle)

situation instead?

A: Your feelings tell you that you _____ to your wife's problem. You're

                                 8. (should / adjust)

right. Adjusting only makes the situation worse. Instead, you _____ her,

                                          9. (ought to / face)

and you _____ to find a solution together. (But see the previous

                   10. (should / try)

question and answer. Don't expect miracles right away!)

Q: Yesterday, my wife had an argument with her boss. I gave her a lot of good strategies for dealing

with her boss, but she didn't listen to me at all, and I felt insulted. _____ I

_____ her problem, or what?

11. (should / ignore)

A: _____. Ignoring your wife wouldn't have been the answer. Next time,

                    12.

try to find out what she wants from you. Maybe she just wants you to listen quietly. She really

_____ you, but since she didn't, try asking directly.

        13. (ought to / tell)

Q: I always make out the checks and pay the bills. It's a very time-consuming process. Last month I

asked my husband to do it because I was busy. He did, but he was angry about it. I feel that he

_____ more pleasantly, but I didn't say anything. _____

        14. (might / act)

I _____?

  15. (should / complain)

A: _____. You were right not to say anything. Remember: You asked him

               16.

to pay the bills, and he did. You didn't ask him to be nice about it.

Q: My husband spends every weekend in front of the TV. He ignores me and the children, and we all

feel bad about that. Last Sunday, he ruined our weekend again. I got upset and called him a couch

potato. What's our problem? I think we _____ solve this before now.

                          17. (ought to / be able to)

A: You're right. He _____ the entire day in front of the TV last Sunday. But

        18. (should / spend)

there are two sides to every problem, and your technique for handling this one made it worse. You

definitely _____ him an insulting name. Name-calling just makes the

        19. (should / call)

situation seem permanent. Instead, you _____ on your own feelings

                       20. (might / focus)

about his actions. You _____ to him that his behavior makes you feel

        21. (could / admit)

insecure and ignored, for example.

EXERCISE 2: Affirmative and Negative Statements

Look at the pointers for resolving conflicts in families. Write sentences about each situation.
Use the words in parentheses and the language from the chart.

Conflicts That Nobody Loses

Situation	Do ...	Don't ...
One of you is a saver, and one is a spender. You fight about money.	• create a budget with some "personal money" for each partner. • treat your partner's attitudes with respect.	• deny your purchases. • accuse your partner of irresponsibility.
You dislike spending time with your spouse's family.	• plan ahead and schedule time alone with each other.	• sulk. • pretend to be sick.
Your child won't clean up his or her room.	• start with small tasks. • provide containers to help organize the toys.	• expect 100 percent change overnight. • yell. • give up and do it yourself.

1. When Tom's wife asked him about a new shirt, he said it wasn't new.

   Tom shouldn't have denied his purchase.
   (should / deny)

2. Cora and Tom planned a budget without any spending money for either of them.

   _____
   (ought to / create)

3. When Cora refused to spend money on a new TV, Tom called her a cheapskate.

   _____
   (might / treat)

4. When Tom bought a new TV anyway, Cora told him he was irresponsible.

   _____
   (should / accuse)

5. On Friday, Kayla and Josh hadn't decided what they were going to do on the weekend. Josh suggested visiting his parents.

   _____
   (should / plan)

6. By Sunday, they hadn't spent any time alone together.

   _____
   (could / schedule)

7. On Saturday, at Kayla's sister's house, Josh wouldn't talk to anybody.

   _____
   (should / sulk)

8. Hakeem's room was a mess. His parents told him to clean the whole room immediately, and Hakeem was very upset.

_____
(might / start)

9. Hakeem didn't know where to put his toys.

_____
(could / provide)

10. Hakeem's father cleaned it up himself on Saturday.

_____
(should / give up / do)

EXERCISE 3: Editing

Read a college student's journal entry. There are nine mistakes in the use of modals. The first mistake is already corrected. Find and correct eight more.

> shouldn't
> I think my new roommate and I have both realized our mistakes. Reggie ~~should~~ have demanded the biggest room in the apartment as soon as he arrived. He ought have spoken to me first—after all, I've lived here longer than he has. On the other hand, I really shouldn't shout at him as soon as he asked me. I could have control my temper and just talked to him about the problem first. I felt really bad about that—until he invited friends over the night before I had to take a test! Then I got so angry I couldn't sleep. He might have asks me first! I oughta have said something right away, but I didn't want to yell again. Of course, some of my habits make Reggie mad too. For example, I could've started washing my dishes when he moved in, but I just let them pile up in the sink. That was pretty gross—I definitely shouldn't have did that. But should have he dumped all the dirty dishes in my bedroom? He might found a better way to tell me he was annoyed. Last week, he wanted to talk about our problems. As soon as we started, I realized we should have tried this technique sooner. Things have worked out a lot better since our discussion.

EXERCISE 4: Personal Writing

Follow the advice of Dr. David Burns (on page 258 of Focus on Grammar 4*). Spend ten minutes writing down all the things that you regret. Use some of the phrases from the box.*

How could I have . . . ?	I ought to have . . .
I could have . . . instead of . . .	I really should have . . .
I might have . . . , but I . . .	I should not have . . .

After you read your list aloud, write a paragraph about whether you agree with Dr. Burns or not. Did the activity help you let go of your regrets? In your paragraph, use some of the phrases from the box.

After I thought about . . .	In my opinion, . . .
From now on, I will . . .	I think writing a list . . .
I still think I could have . . .	Most of my regrets are . . .
In conclusion, . . .	When I said my list of regrets aloud, . . .

Speculations and Conclusions About the Past

EXERCISE 1: Degrees of Probability

Circle the correct words to complete a high school student's notes about the ancient Maya.

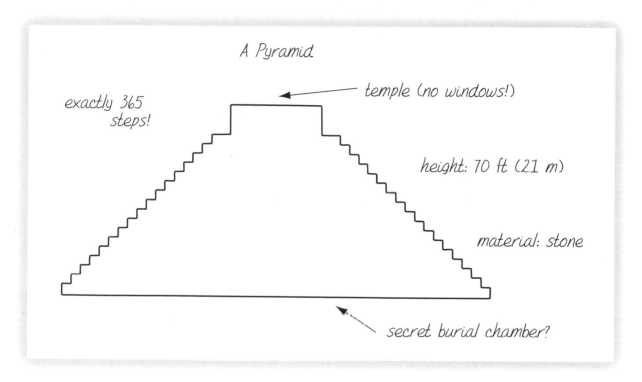

A Pyramid

exactly 365 steps!

temple (no windows!)

height: 70 ft (21 m)

material: stone

secret burial chamber?

1. It **must have** / might have taken many years to build a pyramid.

2. It <u>couldn't have / might not have</u> been easy without horses or oxen.

3. The temples <u>must have / could have</u> been very dark inside.

4. Some pyramids <u>must have / may have</u> had a secret burial chamber.

5. The Maya <u>must have / could have</u> had some knowledge of astronomy.

   Look at the number of steps!

(continued on next page)

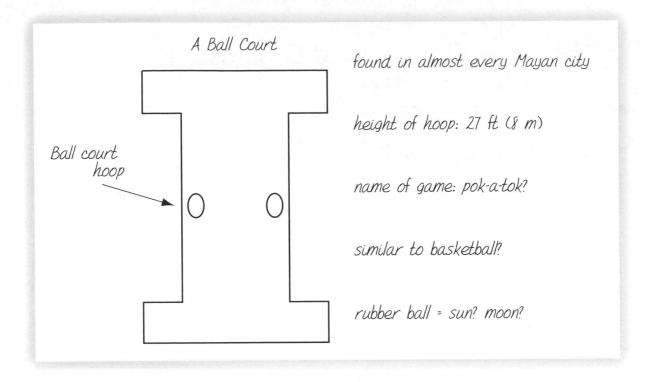

A Ball Court

found in almost every Mayan city

height of hoop: 27 ft (8 m)

name of game: pok-a-tok?

similar to basketball?

rubber ball = sun? moon?

Ball court hoop

6. The Maya <u>must have / might have</u> enjoyed this sport.

7. The name of the game <u>must have / could have</u> been pok-a-tok.

8. It <u>must have / may have</u> been similar to basketball.

9. The solid rubber ball the Maya used <u>must have / could have</u> symbolized the sun or the moon.

10. The average Mayan man was 5 feet 1 inch (1.52 meters) tall. It <u>couldn't have / might not have</u> been very easy to get the ball into the hoop.

11. The rules of the game were complicated. It <u>had to have / might have</u> been very difficult to score points.

EXERCISE 2: Affirmative and Negative Statements

Who were the ancient Maya? What happened to their advanced civilization? Complete the speculations with the verbs in parentheses. Choose between affirmative and negative forms.

1. The ancient Maya _____ *must have been* _____ very intelligent people. They
   (must / be)

   had developed the most complex writing system in the Western Hemisphere as well as an

   amazingly accurate astronomical calendar.

2. In the 1990s, archaeologists found four new Mayan sites in thick mountain jungle

on the Yucatán Peninsula in Mexico. Because of the thick jungle growth, the sites

_____ easily visible.
               (must / be)

3. Archaeologists _____ very excited by the discovery. It
                         (had to / feel)

contributed a lot of important information to their knowledge about the Maya.

4. The Maya _____ the sites between the years 700 and 900.
               (must / occupy)

The style of architecture and the pottery found at the sites are typical of that time.

5. The sites lie between two major population centers. The Maya _____
                                             (may / trade)

with other ancient peoples in their encounters with them.

6. Archaeologists once thought the Maya _____ in the city
                          (could / live)

centers. They believed that the centers were used only for ceremonial purposes.

7. Archaeologists used to believe that the ancient Maya were very peaceful. Today, however,

there is evidence that they _____ as peacefully as people
                               (may / live)

used to believe.

8. Burn marks on buildings, war images on buildings and pottery, and the discovery of weapons

have led archaeologists to the conclusion that the Maya _____
                                                 (must / fight)

in wars.

9. Archaeologist Arthur Demarest believes that after the year 751, there was intense rivalry

among Mayan rulers. He says, "Their ferocious competition, which exploded into civil war,

_____ what finally triggered the society's breakdown."
                (may / be)

10. The rainforests _____ enough food to support the Maya.
                         (might / produce)

Archaeologists have found evidence that at some point the rainforests were almost destroyed.

11. The Maya _____ to other areas in search of food. That
                      (could / go)

would explain their suddenly abandoning their homes.

12. The Maya _____ enough water. There was a four-month
                      (might / have)

dry period every year.

(continued on next page)

13. Some areas _____ from overpopulation. Archaeologist T.
    (may / suffer)

    Patrick Culbert estimates that there were as many as 200 people per square kilometer.

14. Overpopulation _____ to hunger. Human bones show
    (could / lead)

    evidence of poor nutrition.

15. Experts speculate that the Maya had so many problems toward the end of their civilization

    that even a small disaster _____ them.
    (might / destroy)

16. Culbert says the final cause of destruction "_____
    (could / be)

    something totally trivial—two bad hurricane seasons . . . or a crazy king."

EXERCISE 3: Short Answers

Some tourists are talking. Complete the conversations with the correct form of the verbs in
parentheses or with short answers. Choose between affirmative and negative forms.

1. **A:** Those pyramids we saw were fascinating. Do you think they took a long time to build?

   B: _____ *They must have* _____. According to our guide, the Maya didn't have
       (must)

   horses or any other animals to carry the stone.

2. **A:** It was really hot out there today. Do you think it was more than 90 degrees?

   B: _____. Everyone was sweating.
       (must)

3. **A:** The tour guide was really informative. Do you think he's studied archaeology?

   B: _____. He surely knows a lot.
       (might)

4. **A:** I wonder if the guide ever heard of von Däniken's theories.

   B: _____. Von Däniken is pretty well known.
       (may)

5. **A:** I just called Sue's room, and there was no answer. Do you suppose she went out?

   B: _____. She said something about wanting to buy
       (could)

   some postcards to send home.

6. **A:** Do you think pok-a-tok was a rough sport?

   B: _____. The players used to wear thick, heavy padding
       (must)

   for protection.

7. **A:** What did you think of lunch?

   B: It was very good. Did the Maya eat tortillas too?

   A: _____. Their main crop was corn, and archaeologists
   (must)
   have found *metates* in the ruins.

   B: *Metates*? What are those?

   A: Stones used for grinding corn into flour.

8. **A:** The guide didn't say anything about the tip we gave him. Do you think he was happy

   with it?

   B: _____. Maybe we didn't give him enough.
   (might)

9. **A:** I don't feel well.

   B: Do you think it was something you ate?

   A: _____. We ate the exact same thing, and you're fine!
   (could)

EXERCISE 4: Modal Meanings

*Complete the conversations. Use a modal or modal expression from the box and the words
in parentheses. Use the choices from the box only once.*

couldn't have	might have	~~must have~~

1. **A:** I was surprised that Max wasn't taking photos of the pyramids yesterday.

   B: He's been very forgetful lately. He ___*must have left his camera in his room*___.
   (leave his camera in his room)

2. **A:** Is Sue still a student?

   B: I don't know. She _____.
   (finish her degree)

3. **A:** Max went to the top of Pyramid X yesterday.

   B: He _____.
   (climb that pyramid)
   The stairs and all the area around it were closed.

(continued on next page)

may have	might not have	must not have

4. **A:** I didn't see any items from the daily life of the Maya when we visited the pyramids.

   B: The government _____.
   (take everything to the local museum)

5. **A:** Spanish explorers came here in the 1700s, but no one really paid much attention to what

   they found.

   B: They _____.
   (understand the importance of their discoveries)

6. **A:** My guidebook says we know a lot about Mayan civilization because of photographer John

   Lloyd Stephens.

   B: That's right. Without the photos he took of Mayan ruins in the 1840s, researchers

   _____.
   (get so interested in the Maya)

could have	couldn't have	had to have

7. **A:** What was the population of this area in the time of the Maya?

   B: According to our guide, about 6,000. Because of the limited space, there

   _____.
   (be more people)

8. **A:** Did the Maya use math?

   B: I think it's logical, don't you? Their civilization was very advanced. They

   _____.
   (develop a system of numbers)

9. **A:** Can you see what's here on this wall?

   B: It's not really clear. It looks like a Mayan artist

   _____.
   (paint a picture of a warrior)

Read the email from Sue's mother. There are eight mistakes in the use of modals. The first mistake is already corrected. Find and correct seven more.

Dear Sue,

received
I sent you an email last week, but I never heard back from you. You might not have ~~receive~~ it, or you may had been too busy to respond. I understand. It's not easy to keep in touch when you're traveling.

Your father and I got your postcard of the Mayan temple. You had to have enjoyed that part of your trip. I know how interested you are in archeology. I saw a program on television a while ago about the Maya. Actually, it was about the Red Queen. The scientists who found her must not have been really surprised because it was the first time anyone had discovered the body of a Mayan woman in a royal tomb. They're still trying to figure out who she was.

Because she was buried in a way similar to Mayan kings, she must has belonged to the royal family, but that doesn't completely solve the mystery of her identity. The red dust that covered her body made the investigation difficult. At first, scientists thought she could have been one of three women. I found their names on a Red Queen website—Yohl Ik Nal, Zak Kuk, and Tzakbu Ajaw.

After careful research, the scientists decided the woman had lived sometime during the 7th century, which meant it was impossible for her to be Yohl Ik Nal. It might not have been her because Yohl Ik Nal died earlier than that. They also eliminated Zak Kuk, the mother of Pacal II, because the DNA in the body of the Red Queen was different from the DNA in the body of King Pacal II. There was no biological connection between them, so Zak Kuk could have been the Red Queen either. The last woman, Tzakbu Ajaw, must have been the Red Queen, but the researchers don't have enough information to be sure. Tzakbu Ajaw was the mother of Pacal II's children, but their bodies have not been found yet, so there is no DNA to compare.

You might have find out something more about the Red Queen when you visited the Mayan temples. If you did, let me know. But no matter what, please call me, text me, or email me. I miss you!

XXX, OOO,

Mom

EXERCISE 6: Personal Writing

Write one paragraph about an unsolved mystery that you have read or heard about in the news. Use some of the phrases from the box.

Because . . . must not have . . .	One possible explanation was that . . .
I am interested in . . . because . . .	The . . . could have . . .
I found out about the mystery when . . .	The mystery that . . .
Of course, I'm not sure, but I have my own idea about what happened. The . . .	There was no way . . .

UNIT 18 The Passive: Overview

EXERCISE 1: Active and Passive

*Write active and passive sentences. Use **they** in active sentences when you don't know the subject.*

1. (active)   They print the publication monthly.

   (passive)   <u>*The publication is printed monthly.*</u>

2. (active)   <u>*The political editor discovered a serious mistake in the July edition.*</u>

   (passive) A serious mistake was discovered by the political editor in the July edition.

3. (active)   They fired several employees as a result of the mistake.

   (passive) _____

4. (active)   They published an article about the Philippines a decade ago.

   (passive) _____

5. (active) _____

   (passive) The article was written by Al Baker.

6. (active) _____

   (passive) New editors are frequently hired at the magazine.

7. (active)   Two of the new editors interviewed Marla Jacobson.

   (passive) _____

8. (active) _____

   (passive) Marla was given an assignment on the Philippines.

9. (active)   Marla researched the article thoroughly.

   (passive) _____

10. (active) _____

    (passive) Our readers were fascinated by the new article.

EXERCISE 2: Passive Statements: Simple Present and Simple Past

Complete the facts about the Philippines with the passive form of the verbs in parentheses.

1. The Philippines _____*were named*_____ by the Spanish explorer Villalobos in 1543.
   (name)

2. The islands _____ Filipinas to honor the Prince of Asturias, who
   (call)
   later became King Phillip II of Spain.

3. The country _____ by its Spanish name any longer. Its official name
   (not know)
   is the Republic of the Philippines.

4. The nation _____ of 7,100 islands.
   (make up)

5. Only eleven of them _____ major islands.
   (consider)

6. An old legend says that the Philippines _____ when a giant threw a
   (form)
   huge mass of rock into the sea.

7. In reality, the islands _____ by volcanoes.
   (create)

8. Today about 1,000 of the islands _____.
   (populate)

9. Most of the small islands _____.
   (not inhabit)

10. The two large islands of Luzon and Mindanao and the group of small islands between them
    _____ by the three stars on the Philippine flag.
    (represent)

EXERCISE 3: Active or Passive

*Here are some more facts about the Philippines. Complete the sentences with the active or
passive form of the verbs in parentheses.*

1. The Philippines _____*are located*_____ in the tropics.
   (locate)

2. Most people _____*live*_____ near the water.
   (live)

3. However, the mountains _____ too.
   (inhabit)

4. Large rivers _____ on the main islands.
   (find)

5. Floods often _____ roads and bridges.
   (damage)

6. Windstorms _____ property damage and loss of life.
   (cause)

7. Long ago, most of the land _____ by forests.
   (cover)

8. Today, forests _____ over 70,000 square miles.
   (cover)

9. They _____ more than 3,000 kinds of trees.
   (contain)

10. Wild hogs _____ on most of the islands.
    (find)

11. Water buffalo _____ for cultivating the flooded rice fields.
    (use)

12. About 1,000 species of birds and 2,000 species of fish _____ in
    (exist)

    the Philippines.

EXERCISE 4: The Passive: With or Without an Agent

Complete the information about the Philippines. Use the passive form of the verbs in the first set of parentheses. Include the agent in the second set of parentheses only when necessary.

1. When the Spanish explorers came to the Philippines in the 1500s, the islands

   _____ were inhabited by three groups of people _____.
   (inhabit) (three groups of people)

2. The Aëtas _____ *are believed* _____ to be the earliest inhabitants.
   (believe) (people)

3. Thousands of years later, the Aëtas _____.
   (follow) (groups from Indonesia)

4. Today, 8 native languages and almost 90 dialects _____
   (speak) (the Filipinos)

   in the Philippines.

5. Because they are similar, most dialects _____.
   (understand) (speakers of other dialects)

6. On December 31, 1937, Tagalog _____
   (declare) (President Manuel Quezon)

   to be the official language of the Philippines.

7. Today it _____.
   (speak) (more than 70 million people)

8. Tagalog _____ in schools throughout the Philippines.
   (teach) (teachers)

9. Tagalog belongs to the Austronesian family of languages, which _____
   (speak) (people)

   all across the Pacific, from Hawaii to Taiwan.

10. English _____ for commercial and business purposes.
    (use) (people)

Look at this map of Bolivia.

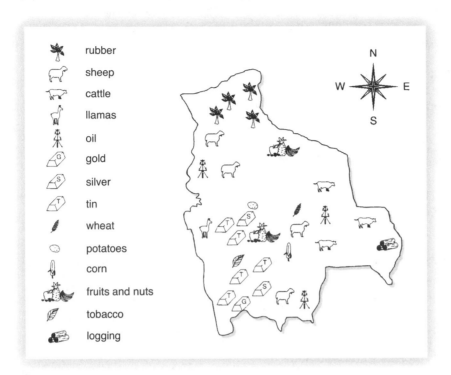

rubber
sheep
cattle
llamas
oil
gold
silver
tin
wheat
potatoes
corn
fruits and nuts
tobacco
logging

Write questions with the passive form of the words. Use the information on the map to answer the questions. Write short answers to **yes / no** *questions and complete sentences for* **wh-** *questions.*

1. tin / mine / in the north?

    A: _Is tin mined in the north?_

    B: _No, it isn't._

2. What other minerals / mine in Bolivia?

    A: _What other minerals are mined in Bolivia?_

    B: _Gold and silver are mined in Bolivia._

3. Where / fruits and nuts / grow?

    A: _____

    B: _____

4. Where / logging / do?

    A: _____

    B: _____

5. What animals / raise?

A: _____

B: _____

6. llamas / find / in the east?

A: _____

B: _____

7. potatoes / grow?

A: _____

B: _____

8. Where / rubber / produce?

A: _____

B: _____

9. Where / oil / find?

A: _____

B: _____

10. wheat / grow / in the north?

A: _____

B: _____

11. cattle / raise / in the east?

A: _____

B: _____

EXERCISE 6: Editing

Read the letter from the editor that appeared at the front of an architecture magazine.
There are eight mistakes in the use of the passive. The first mistake is already corrected.
Find and correct seven more.

Dear Readers:

    Our mission is to bring you the world's great architecture, and in this issue, our spotlight is

focused

~~focus~~ on India. The Taj Mahal, which is locates in northern India, is considered one of the eight

wonders of the world. It was built by builders for the Mughal emperor Shah Jahan. The emperor

was felt great sadness when his wife Mumtaz Mahal died during the birth of their fourteenth child

in 1631, and the Taj Mahal were created as a symbol of his eternal love. The incredible structure,

which was finish in approximately 1653, contains examples of Persian, Islamic, and Indian

architecture, and in 1983, it was became a UNESCO World Heritage Site.

    The romance and beauty of Indian architecture don't stop with the Taj Mahal. Magnificent

buildings found throughout India, and you'll see marvelous examples in the photos and articles in

this issue of our magazine. I'm sure that, like me,

you'll enjoy them all.

Sincerely,

Katarina Wilder

Katarina Wilder

Editor-in-Chief

EXERCISE 7: Personal Writing

On a separate piece of paper, write two paragraphs about a place that you have always
wanted to visit. In the first paragraph, give background information about the place. In the
second paragraph, explain why you'd like to go there. Use some of the phrases from the box.

. . . is known for . . .	It is located . . .
All the photographs that . . .	The . . . was built . . .
I plan . . .	The place that . . .
I really want to visit . . . because . . .	When I go there, I . . .

The Passive with Modals and Similar Expressions

EXERCISE 1: Active and Passive

*Write active and passive sentences. Use **they** in active sentences when you don't know the subject.*

1. (active)   Many countries will build new airports soon.

   (passive) New airports will be built by many countries soon.

2. (active)   They may construct some new airports on islands.

   (passive) _____

3. (active)   _____

   (passive) Passenger facilities might be put on decks under the runways.

4. (active)   They could save a lot of space that way.

   (passive) _____

5. (active)   _____

   (passive) An island airport had to be built in Osaka Bay by the Japanese.

6. (active)   At the old airport, they couldn't handle all the air traffic.

   (passive) _____

7. (active)   They had to move huge amounts of earth from nearby mountains.

   (passive) _____

8. (active)   Hong Kong's island airport will impress international visitors.

   (passive) _____

9. (active)   _____

   (passive) The airport can be reached easily by travelers.

10. (active) Before, they could reach Lantau only by ferry.

   (passive) _____

Complete the article with the correct form of the words in parentheses. Choose between affirmative and negative forms.

BRIDGING CULTURES
by Abdul Santana

While astronauts are working out cultural differences on international space projects, people here on Earth _____*could be brought*_____ closer together than ever before. Engineers
1. (could / bring)

believe that many bodies of land, including continents, _____ by
2. (can / connect)

bridges and tunnels. One of these undertakings has already been completed. Some others

_____ soon. Here's a sampling of the projects and a few of their benefits.
3. (may / start)

England and Europe. The Channel Tunnel between France and England, the first of these

projects, has been operating since 1994. With the "Chunnel," passengers

_____ by train under the English Channel. Unfortunately for driving
4. (can / carry)

enthusiasts, individual cars _____ through the Chunnel. However, there
5. (may / drive)

is a shuttle, and in this way, up to 180 vehicles at a time _____.
6. (are able to / transport)

Africa and Europe. The governments of Spain and Morocco investigated the possibility of a tunnel

under the Straight of Gibraltar but decided that it _____. Still, a bridge
7. (could / do)

connecting the continents of Europe and Africa _____ at some point.
8. (might / build)

In one plan, more than nine miles of water _____ by the structure. New

9. (must / cross)

construction techniques _____ for the bridge because it will be three

10. (have to / develop)

times higher than any bridge built so far.

Asia and Europe. In 2009, the governor of Yunnan Province in China proposed a new land bridge

to connect Asia and Europe. In his plan, a total of 17 countries between Shenzhen, China, and

Rotterdam in the Netherlands _____ by a system of railways and

11. (be going to / link)

highways. Another section _____ to the Eurasian land bridge in the

12. (might / add)

future to include countries in the Middle East and Africa. From the governor's perspective, the land

bridge will improve transportation, increase trade, and save energy.

Asia and North America. According to engineers, small islands located in the Bering Strait

_____ by a bridge carrying a railroad line, a highway, and oil and gas

13. (could / join)

pipelines. If the bridge is built, it _____ the Intercontinental Peace Bridge.

14. (will / call)

Italy and Sicily. Every year, 14 million people cross the Strait of Messina between Sicily and Italy.

These travelers have been promised a bridge and highway for a long time, but this promise

_____ as quickly as people would like. Frequent earthquakes and

15. (might / fulfill)

dangerous winds of more than 125 miles per hour mean that, unfortunately, some delays

_____. These problems _____ promise the

16. (can / avoid)   17. (will / solve)

construction experts who have proposed a 2-mile extension bridge that can withstand both

quakes and high winds.

Complete the interview between EuroTravel *magazine (EM) and Jean-Paul David (JD). Use the correct form of the words in parentheses or short answers where appropriate.*

EM: I'd like to ask a question about taking cars through the Chunnel on Le Shuttle.

_____Do_____ cars _____have to be occupied_____ during the trip?
1. (have to / occupy)

JD: _____. Drivers can get out and walk alongside their vehicles if they
2.

feel like it.

EM: Now, what about the regular passenger train—the Eurostar? _____ tickets

_____ in advance?
3. (should / obtain)

JD: _____. It's best to have a reservation. Most passengers also need to
4.

check in at least 30 minutes before the train departs.

EM: And _____ the reservations _____ online?
5. (can / make)

JD: _____. In fact, that's probably the most efficient way to book a trip.
6.

EM: Then _____ tickets _____ to travelers?
7. (will / mail)

JD: _____. Eurostar is doing what it can to protect the environment. The
8.

process is completely electronic.

EM: A lot of our readers are interested in skiing. _____ train service to the Alps

_____ again this year?
9. (be going to / offer)

JD: _____. Both day trains and night trains equipped with sleeping
10.

accommodations have been scheduled for the ski season.

EM: _____ food _____ aboard the Eurostar ski trains?
11. (can / purchase)

JD: _____. There are bar-buffet cars offering a selection of both hot and
12.

cold food.

EM: Sounds good. Thanks. This information will be appreciated by our readers.

Read the article about space tourism. There are eight mistakes in the use of passive with modals and similar expressions. The first mistake is already corrected. Find and correct seven more.

TRAVEL

Space Tourism May Not Be So Far Away

be

If you like to reach for the stars when it comes to travel, you may~interested in a trip to space. Of course, your choices for space travel will be limit by the amount of money you can spend, but there's something for everyone.

Space tourism became a reality in 2001 for travelers with big bank accounts. The more than $20 million cost of a trip to the International Space Station could paid only by millionaires like U.S. businessman Dennis Tito or Canadian Guy Laliberté, the founder of Cirque du Soleil. Now comes the news that tourists will be taking into suborbital space by Virgin Galactic. The six travelers and two pilots on the Virgin Galactic flights can't remain in space for an extended period of time, and their spaceship won't orbit the Earth. However, they will be shoot by a rocket to a height of 68 miles, where there will be a true outer space experience. At that height, the blackness of space can be seen and in it the curved shape of the planet Earth. Spacesuits must been worn at all times, but seat belts can be removed for about four or five minutes to allow travelers to enjoy the feeling of floating in zero gravity. According to reports, 335 tickets at a cost of $200,000 each have already been reserved.

If $200,000 is still beyond your budget, your dreams of an out-of-this-world experience have to be forgotten. A half-day "Astronaut Training Experience" is available at NASA's Kennedy Space Center near Orlando, Florida, for $145. Even better, your name can put on a microchip that is part of a future NASA research project for free. Go to NASA's website for more information.

On a separate piece of paper, write a paragraph that gives your opinion about whether or not space tourism is a good idea. Use some of the phrases from the box.

I feel very strongly that space tourism has to be . . .	On the positive side, . . .
In the future, space tourism . . .	The best reason that . . .
On the negative side, . . .	The cost of space tourism . . .

The Passive Causative

EXERCISE 1: Passive Causatives

Rewrite the sentences using the passive causative. Include the agent only when necessary.

1. Someone does my taxes every April.

   I have my taxes done every April.

2. Someone is repairing my computer.

   _____

3. My favorite mechanic at Majestic Motors checked my car.

   _____

4. Someone has just cleaned our windows.

   _____

5. Someone is going to cut our grass.

   _____

6. Someone must paint our house.

   _____

7. Someone should check our electrical wiring.

   _____

8. Northtown Contractors will probably do most of the work on our house.

   _____

9. They might build a new porch for us too.

   _____

10. Someone had better remove the dead tree from the neighbors' yard.

    _____

Complete the article about consumer fraud. Use the passive causative form of the verbs in parentheses.

Getting a Charge for Nothing

by Selma Johnson

After an event such as an earthquake or a flood, consumers should be prepared to protect

themselves against dishonest businesses. As a result of damage to their homes, families must

_____*get*_____ major repairs _____*done*_____ quickly. Working under great stress,
1. (get / do)

they sometimes _____ jobs _____ without looking carefully at all
2. (have / complete)

their options or taking the time to get a written estimate first. Often they _____

work _____ by dishonest electricians and other contractors because they haven't
3. (have / do)

checked with the Better Business Bureau. The following is an example.

After a major earthquake in Los Angeles, many people wanted to _____ their

electric wiring systems _____. One electrician told a woman that she had to
4. (get / test)

_____ her circuit breakers _____ to avoid permanent damage to
5. (have / replace)

her home and charged her $510 per breaker. The same breaker cost just $21.86 apiece in a

hardware store. A news show decided to _____ the story _____.
6. (have / investigate)

Using a hidden camera, reporters and camera crews filmed the electrician's visit to another

customer. This customer had a broken circuit breaker, so he _____ a new circuit

breaker _____ to replace it. But the electrician told him that he should also
7. (have / install)

_____ five other circuit breakers _____. And he charged $356 per
8. (get / replace)

breaker. Furthermore, the electrician said that if the customer _____ the job

_____ immediately, there was a risk of fire. The investigative news team
9. (not have / do)

_____ the "broken" circuit breakers _____. Not only did they not
10. (have / test)

need replacement, but the electrician went on to resell the "bad" breakers to other customers.

(continued on next page)

Of course, the majority of workers are honest. But how can you, the consumer, guard against those who aren't? Here are some guidelines:

Be a smart consumer.

Do business only with service people who have good reputations. Before hiring unknown professionals, _____ them _____ by appropriate agencies to see
11. (have / check out)
that they are properly licensed. And although the Better Business Bureau will not make recommendations, they will tell you if they have received any complaints about a company.

Use a credit card if you can.

This way, if there is any problem, you will be able to _____ payment

_____ until the issue is resolved. Your credit card company will even help you
12. (have / stop)
try to resolve the conflict.

Get an estimate.

Always try to get an estimate, and _____ it _____ in writing.
13. (have / put)

Know where to go for help.

If you think you have been a victim of fraud, notify your state Attorney General's Office. In many cities, newspaper and TV reporters also specialize in helping consumers. If they can't help, you will at least have the satisfaction of _____ the problem _____.
14. (get / publicize)

Tyler is talking to his friend Frank about his car. Use the words in parentheses and the passive causative to write Frank's questions.

1. **FRANK:** My old Ford's been giving me trouble lately.

   Where do you usually get your car serviced?
   (Where / usually / get / your car / service)

   TYLER: I always go to Majestic Motors.

2. **FRANK:** _____
   (How often / get / it / do)

   TYLER: Oh, about every 5,000 miles. In fact, I was there just yesterday.

3. **FRANK:** Really?

   _____
   (get / it / winterize)

   TYLER: Well, they put antifreeze in the radiator.

4. **FRANK:** _____
   (ever / get / snow tires / put on)

   TYLER: No, I haven't. We really don't get enough snow around here for that. But we *are* going

   to take a trip to Canada this winter.

5. **FRANK:** _____
   (get / snow tires / put on / for the trip)

   TYLER: I guess it's not a bad idea.

6. **FRANK:** You bought your car in 2008. Right?

   _____
   (How many times / get / it / check / since then)

   TYLER: I can't say exactly. I do a lot of driving, so I've taken it in a lot.

7. **FRANK:** And you always go to Majestic for repairs and maintenance?

   _____
   (Why / get / the work / do / there)

   TYLER: The guy who owns it is a good mechanic, and I trust him. He'd never rip me off.

   FRANK: OK. I think I'll bring my car in and have them take a look at it.

   TYLER: You won't be sorry.

   FRANK: Thanks for the recommendation.

Frank took his car to Majestic Motors. Look at a portion of the checklist of services. Write all the things Frank had or didn't have done. Use the passive causative with **have** *or* **get**.

Majestic Motors

2680 Midlothian Tpke. (corner of Douglas Ave.) • Paramus, OH 45455 • (937) 555-3485

- -

[✓] check tire pressure   [ ] replace air filter

[ ] change oil   [ ] rotate tires

[ ] inspect undercarriage   [ ] adjust timing and engine speed

[✓] lubricate body and chassis [✓] service automatic transmission

[✓] inspect air filter   [✓] flush cooling system

1. *He had the tire pressure checked.*

2. *He didn't have the oil changed.*

3. _____

4. _____

5. _____

6. _____

7. _____

8. _____

9. _____

10. _____

EXERCISE 5: Editing

Read the email. There are nine mistakes in the use of the passive causative. The first mistake is already corrected. Find and correct eight more.

Dear Petra,

       had

We've just ~~have~~ our furniture brought over from the apartment, and we're really excited about moving into our "new" (but very old) house. A 19th-century millionaire had this place build for his daughter by a builder. We were able to afford it because it's a real "fixer-upper." It needs to has a lot of work done. We've already gotten the roof fix, but we're not having the outside painting until fall. The plumbers are doing some work now. It's a complicated procedure, but they should finish soon. After we get repaired the plumbing, we'll paint the inside ourselves (we can't paint over those big water stains until the plumbers leave). It sounds awful, but just wait until you see it. There's a fireplace in every bedroom—we're get the chimneys cleaned before winter. And the windows are huge. In fact, they're so large that we can't wash them ourselves, so yesterday we had done them professionally.

    As you can imagine, we've both been pretty busy, but we'd love to see you. Are you brave enough to visit us?

Love,

Latoya and Vince

EXERCISE 6: Personal Writing

On a separate piece of paper, write a paragraph about a repair problem that you have experienced. For example, the problem could have been with a car repair, computer repair, or work at your home. Use some of the phrases from the box.

According to the repairperson, I had to have . . .	I was finally able to . . .
Here's what I learned from my experience. I . . .	The next time . . .
I had a huge problem when . . .	The only way that I could get my . . .
I tried to get . . . , but . . .	The problem continued for . . .

UNIT 21   Present Real Conditionals

EXERCISE 1: Simple Present

Look at the schedule of airplane fares. Then read the statements. For each statement, write **That's right** *or* **That's wrong**. *If the statement is wrong, correct the underlined information.*

AIR ITALY ✈ SUPER BARGAIN AIRFARES Destination: Rome				
GATEWAY	OFF SEASON*		PEAK**	
	Round Trip	One Way	Round Trip	One Way
New York	$745	$475	$889	$559
Boston	$745	$475	$889	$559
Philadelphia	$769	$489	$915	$569
Washington	$769	$489	$915	$569
Chicago	$809	$505	$949	$589
Cincinnati	$809	$505	$949	$589
Atlanta	$829	$519	$975	$599

*Off Season: 4/1–5/31 and 10/1–10/31; **Peak: 6/1–9/30

1. If you leave from New York in April, you pay $475 for a <u>round-trip</u> ticket.

   That's wrong. If you leave from New York in April, you pay $475 for a one-way ticket.

2. If you leave from Boston in June, you pay $559 for a <u>one-way</u> ticket.

   That's right.

3. You pay <u>more</u> if you leave from Chicago than if you leave from New York.

   _____

4. If you travel in September, your ticket costs <u>less</u> than if you travel in October.

   _____

5. If you fly in May, you pay <u>peak</u>-season rates.

   _____

6. If you buy a one-way ticket, you pay <u>half</u> the cost of a round-trip ticket.

_____

7. If you fly round trip from <u>Atlanta</u> in October, the ticket price is $829.

_____

8. If you fly from Chicago, the fare is <u>the same as</u> from Cincinnati.

_____

9. If you leave from <u>Boston</u>, you pay the same fare as from Philadelphia.

_____

10. If you fly from Philadelphia, you pay a <u>higher</u> fare than from Chicago.

_____

EXERCISE 2: Imperatives and Modals

Read the conversations about traveling to Italy. Write conditional sentences to summarize the travel agent's advice. Begin each sentence with **if**.

1. **TOURIST:** We're thinking of going to Italy.

    AGENT: You should book a flight now.

    SUMMARY: _If you're thinking of going to Italy, you should book a flight now._

    Things fill up early in the summer.

2. **TOURIST:** We're flexible.

    AGENT: Don't go in the summer.

    SUMMARY: _If you're flexible, don't go in the summer._

    It's very hot and crowded in the summer. Besides, the rates are higher.

3. **TOURIST:** We don't want to spend a lot of money getting around in Rome.

    AGENT: Take public transportation.

    SUMMARY: _____

    Taxis are expensive. You can get around fine with buses and trains.

4. **TOURIST:** We want to be smart consumers when we book this trip.

    AGENT: Get a package deal with both airfare and hotel included.

    SUMMARY: _____

    It's a sure way to save money.

(continued on next page)

5. TOURIST: We prefer small hotels.

   AGENT: Stay at a *pensione*.

   SUMMARY: _____

   It's usually more intimate and personal than a hotel.

6. TOURIST: My husband is very interested in architecture.

   AGENT: You must visit the Palazzo Ducale in Venice.

   SUMMARY: _____

   It's a gorgeous building made of pink-and-white marble. You can find a photo on this website.

7. TOURIST: We love opera.

   AGENT: You should attend an open-air performance in Verona's Roman Arena.

   SUMMARY: _____

   It's just a short distance from Venice.

8. TOURIST: I'm interested in seeing ancient ruins.

   AGENT: You might want to consider a side trip to Ostia Antica.

   SUMMARY: _____

   The ruins there are as interesting as the ones in Pompeii, and they're only a 30-minute train ride from Rome.

9. TOURIST: We plan to take a hair dryer and an electric shaver with us.

   AGENT: Don't forget to take a transformer and an adapter.

   SUMMARY: _____

   The electricity varies considerably in Italy, and unlike in the United States and Canada, outlets have round holes.

10. TOURIST: We want to have a really good dinner our first night there.

   AGENT: You should try Sabatini's.

   SUMMARY: _____

   It's one of the most popular restaurants in Rome. I hear that the spaghetti with seafood is excellent.

Complete the article about health advice for travelers. Combine the two sentences to make a real conditional sentence. Keep the same order and decide which clause begins with **if**. Make necessary changes in capitalization and punctuation.

If You Go, Go Safely

It can happen. You're miles away from home on vacation or a business trip and you feel sick. What should you do? Here are some tips from travel experts.

1. (You travel. You need to take special health precautions.)

   If you travel, you need to take special health precautions.

A little preplanning can go a long way in making your trip a healthier one.

2. (Don't pack medication in your luggage. You plan to check your luggage on the plane.)

   Don't pack medication in your luggage if you plan to check your luggage on the plane.

Keep it in your carry-on bags. That way, if the airline loses your luggage, you won't be left without your medicine.

3. (You should bring along copies of your prescriptions and keep them in a secure place. You take prescription medication.)

   _____

   _____

Make sure they are written in the generic (not the brand-name) form.

4. (Notify the flight attendant or train conductor. You feel sick on board a plane or train.)

   _____

   _____

They are trained to deal with the situation.

(*continued on next page*)

5. (Call your own doctor. You are traveling in your own country when you feel sick.)

_____

_____

He or she may be able to refer you to a doctor in the area.

6. (Your hotel can recommend a doctor. You need medical attention in a foreign country.)

_____

_____

As an alternative, you can contact your embassy or consulate.

7. (You experience chest pains, weakness in an arm or leg, or shortness of breath. Get yourself to an emergency room.)

_____

_____

These can be symptoms of a heart attack. Time is of the utmost importance.

8. (You're not sure how serious your symptoms are. Assume they are serious and take appropriate steps.)

_____

_____

It's better to be safe than sorry. Many travelers tend to ignore symptoms when they are away from home.

9. (Don't drive to the hospital. You need to go to the emergency room.)

_____

_____

It's easy to get lost in an unfamiliar location. Take a taxi instead.

10. (You wear glasses. Take an extra pair with you.)

_____

_____

Many a vacation has been ruined by this lack of foresight.

Have a safe trip!

Read the tips about airline travel that a travel agent prepared for her clients. There are nine mistakes in the use of present real conditionals. The first mistake is already corrected. Find and correct eight more. Don't forget to check punctuation.

SUPER BARGAINS TRAVEL, INC.
The Truth About Airline Travel

➤ You ~~had~~ *have* a better chance of getting a good seat on the plane if you buy your ticket early.

➤ If you took a nonstop flight, it is sometimes cheaper than a trip with plane changes. It's *when* you travel that really counts. Your schedule is flexible, if you should take advantage of travel at off-peak hours.

➤ Be aware of airline policy about cancellations or changes in reservations. When you make a change in your travel plans, there are almost always extra fees.

➤ If you do online check-in from your home or hotel the amount of time you stand in line at the airport decreases. Besides, you know that your seat on the plane is confirmed, if you have a boarding pass before arriving at the airport.

➤ You save both time and money when you travel light. You don't have to wait in line to check a bag before departure or pick it up at baggage claim if you has just a carry-on bag and one personal item. Even better, if you bring no luggage to check, then there are no baggage fees to pay.

➤ Airline employees try to be helpful they see problems. However, there is sometimes nothing they can do. If you needed to dispute anything, be as polite as possible. It's the best way to get great service.

➤ If you travel often, then you know what I mean with this next piece of advice. Wear shoes that you can take off and put on easily. Frequent fliers use this strategy to make things easier at the security checkpoint.

➤ If you're traveling internationally, you must have your passport and visa documents with you. Even if they are traveling in their own country, many experienced travelers are carrying their passport. It's the safest form of personal identification.

EXERCISE 5: Personal Writing

Write a paragraph with your most important piece of advice for travelers. Use some of the phrases from the box.

As a general rule, if . . .	If you want . . .
If I go on a trip, . . .	In my opinion, travelers should . . . if . . .
If you . . . , you should not . . .	When I . . .
If you are a smart traveler, . . .	You can . . . if . . .

EXERCISE 1: *If* and *Unless*, **Affirmative and Negative, Simple Present and Future**

Circle the correct words to complete this Internet health and fitness quiz. (Note: You can find the answers to the quiz in Exercise 3.)

HEALTH AND FITNESS QUIZ
Fact or Fiction?
How much do you really know about health and fitness?
Put your knowledge to the test.

	Fact	Fiction
1. **If** / Unless you want to be thin, you will have to watch your **a.** calorie intake.	○	○
2. If you <u>skip / will skip</u> a meal, you'll eat fewer calories each **b.** day, so you'll lose weight.	○	○
3. It will be difficult for you to lose weight and keep it off <u>if / unless</u> you <u>exercise / will exercise</u> regularly. **c.** **d.**	○	○
4. Carrots are good for your eyesight. <u>If / Unless</u> you eat **e.** them, your vision will improve.	○	○
5. If you <u>change / will change</u> your eating habits and become **f.** a vegetarian, you <u>are / will be</u> healthier. **g.**	○	○
6. If you <u>take / will take</u> vitamin C daily, you <u>catch / won't catch</u> **h.** **i.** a cold.	○	○
7. If your body <u>has / will have</u> too much vitamin A, you might **j.** experience health problems.	○	○

(continued on next page)

	Fact	Fiction
8. You are <u>having / going to have</u> trouble staying healthy _{k.} <u>if / unless</u> you drink eight glasses of water a day. _{l.}	○	○
9. <u>If / Unless</u> you <u>go / will go</u> outside with wet hair when the _{m.} _{n.} weather is cold, you'll get sick.	○	○

SUBMIT

EXERCISE 2: Conditional Questions and Responses: Affirmative and Negative

Complete the conversation with the correct form of the words in parentheses or with short answers.

Raúl: I'm shocked by the number of people who believe everything they read on the Internet. They

should realize that if they _____ *use* _____ the Web, they're going to see a lot of
1. (use)

information that may not be true.

Yan: What do you mean?

Raúl: At the moment, there is widespread use of the Internet. There are millions of sites and in the

not-too-distant future there are going to be lots more. Anyone can put up a website.

Yan: That's an interesting insight. I've never really thought about it before, but you're right.

I'll be doing a project for my writing class soon. If I _____
2. (decide)

to use the Internet for my research, how _____ I

_____ about the accuracy of a website?
3. (know)

Raúl: First of all, consider the source. In other words, if you _____ to
4. (go)

the sites of well-respected organizations, they _____ probably

_____ reliable information.
5. (have)

Yan: _____ I _____ figure out who a website
6. (be able to)

belongs to if I _____ somewhere on the site?
7. (look)

RAÚL: _____ 8. . Look for an "About us" link on the home page. Most

websites, especially legitimate ones, will provide this kind of information, and unless you

_____ 9. (have) it, you _____ 10. (not be) confident about a

site's reliability.

YAN: Is there anything else I should look for?

RAÚL: If a Web address _____ 11. (end) with ".edu" or ".org," you

_____ probably _____ 12. (find) good information

there.

YAN: If I _____ 13. (see) ".com" as part of the address,

_____ that _____ 14. (tell) me anything?

RAÚL: _____ 15. . A ".com" extension will usually be used by people or

businesses selling a product. The information on these commercial sites can be useful, but its

purpose might be to sell rather than inform.

YAN: I understand. Now, what can you tell me about Internet hoaxes?

RAÚL: They're quite common. Unless you _____ 16. (set) the junk mail filter to keep

them out of your email, you _____ 17. (receive) one sometime soon.

YAN: If one of these messages _____ 18. (show up) in my email,

_____ it _____ 19. (be) difficult to recognize?

RAÚL: _____ 20. . An email hoax will be easy for you to spot.

YAN: How?

RAÚL: Most of them will make ridiculous claims. According to one hoax, if people

_____ 21. (wash) their hair with certain kinds of shampoo, they

_____ 22. (get) cancer. Hoaxes will also claim to be true, and they'll use lots of

capital letters and exclamation points.

YAN: What if I reply to the senders and ask them to stop sending me messages?

RAÚL: Bad idea. If you _____ 23. (want) to be a smart computer user, you

_____ 24. (not do) anything except delete all junk mail, including

hoaxes, immediately.

Here are the answers to the Internet quiz in Exercise 1. How many questions did you answer correctly? Use the words in parentheses and **if** *or* **unless** *to write future real conditional sentences. Keep the same order as the items in parentheses, and decide where to put* **if** *or* **unless***. Add punctuation where necessary.*

1. Statement 1 is fact.

   <u>You will be able to control your weight more easily if you limit your calorie intake.</u>
   (you / be able to control / your weight more easily) (you / limit / your calorie intake)

   There's a direct connection between your weight and how many calories there are in the food you eat.

2. Statement 2 is fiction.

   <u>If you don't eat a meal, you'll be hungrier at your next meal.</u>
   (you / not / eat / a meal) (you / be / hungrier at your next meal)

   Then you'll overeat, and this will cause you to gain rather than lose weight.

3. Statement 3 is fact.

   _____

   _____
   (you / have / trouble losing weight) (you / get / regular exercise)

   Physical exercise will burn calories and increase your metabolism, which will speed up weight loss and help you keep the pounds (or kilos) off.

4. Statement 4 is fiction.

   _____

   _____
   (you / receive / some health benefits) (you / eat / carrots)

   However, they won't improve poor eyesight.

5. Statement 5 is fiction.

   _____

   _____
   (you / stop eating meat) (you / need / something to replace it in your diet)

   Some vegetarians end up eating a lot of dairy products such as cheese or foods like rice and pasta that have too many calories.

6. Statement 6 is fiction.

_____

_____
(you / have a cold) (vitamin C / help relieve the symptoms)

However, according to recent research, vitamin C can't prevent colds.

7. Statement 7 is fact.

_____

_____
(you / suffer / possible negative effects) (your body / get / too much vitamin A)

Some doctors now believe that an excess of vitamin A can cause bones to weaken and break. It's a good idea to talk to your physician about any vitamin supplements that you plan to take.

8. Statement 8 is fiction.

_____

_____
(you / not / get sick) (you / not / drink / exactly eight glasses of water a day)

Sure, your body needs plenty of water, but the specific amount varies from person to person. Besides, you can get water from other kinds of drinks and from the food that you eat.

9. Statement 9 is fiction.

_____

_____
(you / not / have a problem going out with wet hair) (you / be / worried about feeling cold or looking less than perfect)

It's just a myth that you can get sick by going out in the cold when your hair is wet.

Read the article from the website of a news magazine. There are eight mistakes in the use of future real conditionals. The first mistake is already corrected. Find and correct seven more. Don't forget to check punctuation.

■ WOMEN'S HEALTH ■

Scientists Connect Positive Attitude and Health

If you ~~will~~ want to be healthy, then you should stay positive. At least that's what new medical findings seem to say. According to researchers, if you handle stress well and have an attitude toward life that is positive overall, you won't live a longer, healthier life. In a recent study, adults were asked questions about stressful situations that they were unable to anticipate. For example, they might have been asked, "How you will react if you are stuck in traffic?" or "What will you do if your boss will ask you to start a big project right at the end of the day?" Researchers found that the people with enthusiastic and positive responses had fewer heart attacks over the next 10 years. In a similar study, scientists discovered that having a positive attitude toward the future made people 12 percent less likely to suffer a heart attack. Other research has also shown a connection between a positive attitude and good health. According to the studies, if people will approach life in a positive way, they'll be less likely to get a cold or the flu and more likely to have lower blood pressure.

Will a woman live longer if she develops a more positive attitude? Doctors won't really know if more research is done, but many believe it's possible that a change in attitude will help. Doctors are confident of one thing. You'll feel mentally stronger you do things that you enjoy. So, if you like spending time with friends or playing sports you should do it. And while you're at it, take care of yourself. If you get enough sleep, exercise, and eat right, you'll feel the connection between better health and a more positive attitude.

EXERCISE 5: Personal Writing

Write a paragraph about what you plan to do to improve your health. Use some of the phrases from the box.

I know that I should . . . if . . .	If I don't . . .
I will be able to . . .	It will not be easy, but if . . .
I will feel healthier if . . .	To improve my health, I plan . . .
If . . . , I might . . .	Unless . . . , I will not . . .

EXERCISE 1: Conditionals: Affirmative and Negative

Complete the fairy tale. Use the correct form of the verbs in parentheses.

Stone Soup

𝒪nce upon a time, there were three soldiers. They were on their way home from the wars, and they were very hungry and very tired.

"I wish we _____*had*_____ something good to eat," said the first soldier.
1. (have)

"And I wish we _____ in a nice warm bed," said the second.
2. (can / sleep)

"I wish those things _____ possible," said the third. "But they are not. We must
3. (be)

march on until we reach home."

So on they marched. Suddenly they came to a village. The villagers saw them coming. They knew that soldiers are always hungry. But the villagers didn't have much food. They worried that if they _____ some food to the soldiers, then they themselves
4. (offer)

_____ that night. So they decided to hide all their food.
5. (not eat)

The three soldiers went to the first house. They asked, "Could you give us something to eat and a place to sleep?"

The villagers responded, "We _____ glad to give you food if we
6. (be)

_____ some. But we don't. And we _____ you space to sleep if
7. (have)   8. (give)

we _____ all of it ourselves. But all our beds are full."
9. (not need)

And so it went with all the villagers. Everyone had a good excuse.

"We gave all our food to the soldiers who came before you."

"Our father's sick. We _____ you food if he _____ sick."
10. (offer)   11. (not be)

"The harvest was bad, and we need the grain for cattle feed. If we _____ the
12. (not need)

grain, we _____ it with you."
13. (share)

When the soldiers saw that the villagers refused to grant their requests, they thought, and then they said, "We wish you _____ us something to eat, but since you can't—well,
14. (can / offer)

we'll have to make stone soup."

"Stone soup?" The villagers had never heard of it before.

"First, we'll need a large pot," said the soldiers.

The villagers consented and brought them the largest pot they could find.

"Now we need water to fill it and a fire to cook with."

The villagers brought buckets of water and built a fire in the village square.

"Now we need three round, smooth stones."

That too was no problem at all. The villagers brought them, and the soldiers dropped them into the pot.

The soldiers stirred the pot and added some salt and pepper (all good soups have salt and pepper).

(*continued on next page*)

"Stones like these usually make a very fine soup, but if we _____ some carrots,
                                                          15. (have)

it _____ a lot better," they said.
      16. (taste)

"I think I can find a carrot!" said one of the villagers. She ran home and got all the carrots she

had hidden from the soldiers.

"This soup _____ so much better if we _____ some cabbage in
              17. (taste)   18. (put)

it," said the soldiers as they sliced the carrots. "We wish you _____ some cabbage.
                                                                    19. (have)

It's a shame that you don't."

"Let me see if I can find one," said another villager. She went home and came back with three

cabbages that she had hidden from the soldiers.

"If we _____ a little beef and a few potatoes, this soup _____
          20. (add)   21. (be)

good enough for a rich man's table."

No sooner said than done. The villagers ran to get the hidden food.

Just imagine! A rich man's soup—and all from just a few stones!

The soldiers continued cooking and sighed, "If we _____ in a little barley and a
                                                        22. (stir)

cup of milk, this soup _____ fit for the king himself."
                          23. (be)

The villagers were really impressed. The soldiers knew the king! They wished that *they*

_____ the king!
      24. (know)

The villagers brought their hidden barley and milk to the soldiers, who stirred the ingredients

into the pot.

Finally the soup was ready. Tables were set up in the square, and torches were lit. The soup was

delicious. Fit for a king. But the villagers said to themselves, "If a king _____ this
                                                                              25. (eat)

soup, he _____ bread, and a roast, and some cider to go with it, wouldn't he?"
            26. (require)

Before not too long, everyone sat down to enjoy a great feast of roast, bread, cider, and soup.

Never before had they tasted such delicious soup. And imagine—

it was made just from stones!

EXERCISE 2: *Wish*: Affirmative and Negative Statements

Read the complaints by the villagers in the "Stone Soup" story. Rewrite the complaints as wishes.

1. We don't have enough food.

   We wish we had enough food. _____

2. The soldiers will keep asking for our food.

   _____

3. We have to hide our food from them.

   _____

4. We need all our grain to feed the cows.

   _____

5. All our beds are full.

   _____

6. There isn't enough room for the soldiers.

   _____

7. The king won't come here to eat with us.

   _____

8. We don't have a larger soup pot.

   _____

9. We can't have stone soup every day.

   _____

EXERCISE 3: Conditionals: Affirmative and Negative

*Rewrite the excuses, using the present and future unreal conditional. Begin each sentence with **if**.*

1. We don't have food. That's why we can't feed the soldiers.

   If we had food, we could feed the soldiers. _____

2. I don't have potatoes. That's why I'm not going to make potato soup.

   _____

(continued on next page)

3. My apartment is small. That's why I won't invite people over.

_____

4. Steak is expensive. That's why we don't eat it.

_____

5. My daughter is sick. That's why I won't go shopping later today.

_____

6. I have bad eyesight. That's why I can't join the army.

_____

7. The soup doesn't have seasoning in it. That's why it tastes so bland.

_____

8. I don't know the answer. That's why I'm embarrassed now.

_____

9. I'm not rich. That's why I don't take vacations.

_____

10. I don't have the recipe. That's why I don't make stone soup.

_____

EXERCISE 4: Giving Advice with *If I were you . . .*

Complete the conversations. Use **were** *and the correct form of the verbs in parentheses to write present and future unreal conditionals giving advice. Begin each sentence with* **if.**

1. A: I don't know how to cook.

   B: _If I were you, I'd learn how to cook._____
                              (learn)

      It's an important skill to have.

2. A: I've never read a fairy tale.

   B: _____
                              (read)

      They're a lot of fun.

3. A: I've never tried cabbage soup.

   B: _____
                              (try)

      It's delicious, and it's healthy.

4. A: This soup tastes bland. Where's the salt?

B: _____
   (not add)

   Put some pepper in, instead.

5. A: I'm going to ask for a raise.

B: _____
   (not ask)

   You've only worked here a month.

6. A: *Rambo VII* is playing at the Cineplex. My daughter loves going to the movies.

B: _____
   (not take)

   It's too violent.

7. A: My landlord just raised the rent again.

B: _____
   (move)

   You can find a nice apartment for much less.

8. A: I'm exhausted, and I have no idea what to make for dinner.

B: _____
   (eat out)

   The place across the street has good food, and it's not expensive.

EXERCISE 5: *Yes / No* and *Wh-* Questions

Several campers are sitting around a fire. Write their questions using the present and future unreal conditional.

1. What / we / do / if / we / can't find the way back?

   What would we do if we couldn't find the way back?
   _____

2. Who / look for us / if / we / get lost?

   _____

3. Where / we / go / if / it / start to rain?

   _____

4. you / be afraid / if / we / see a bear?

   _____

5. If / you / hear a loud growl / you / be scared?

   _____

(continued on next page)

6. What / you / do / if / you / be in my place?

_____

7. What / we / do / if / we / run out of food?

_____

8. If / we / not have any more food / we / make stone soup?

_____

EXERCISE 6: Editing

Read the camper's journal entry. There are nine mistakes in the use of present and future unreal conditionals. The first mistake is already corrected. Find and correct eight more.

> 11:00 P.M. June 11
> Somewhere in the forest
> (and it's not enchanted!)
>
> It's 11:00 P.M. and I'm still awake. I wish I ~~was~~ _were_ home. If I would be home, I would be asleep by now! But here I am in the middle of nowhere. I'm furious at myself for agreeing to go camping. My sleeping bag is really uncomfortable. If I were more comfortable, I will be able to sleep. What do my family think if they could see me now?
>
> I'm cold, tired, and hungry. I wish I have something to eat. But all the food is locked up in the van, and everyone else is sound asleep. If I would have a book, I would read, but I didn't bring any books. Tonight, as we sat around the campfire, someone read a story called "Stone Soup." I'm so hungry that even stone soup sounds good to me. If I know the recipe, I made it.
>
> Well, I'm getting tired of holding this flashlight (I wish I would have a regular lamp!), so I think I'll try to fall asleep.

Write a paragraph about one thing that you would do to help others if you had the time and money. Use some of the phrases from the box.

> I could . . . if . . .
>
> I wish . . .
>
> I would . . . if I had . . .
>
> If everyone did just one thing to help those in need, . . .
>
> If I were . . .
>
> People who need help probably wish . . .
>
> The world might . . . if . . .
>
> To help others, I would . . .

EXERCISE 1: *If* and Result Clauses: Verb Forms

Complete the sentences about Mickey Mouse and his creator Walt Disney. Use the correct form of the verbs in parentheses.

1. Walt Disney argued with his bosses at Universal Pictures

   about a cartoon character named Oswald the Lucky Rabbit.

   If Disney _____**hadn't argued**_____ with his bosses, he
   (not argue)

   _____**wouldn't have left**_____ Universal Pictures in 1928.
   (not leave)

2. Walt Disney had to come up with an alternate plan after his

   departure from Universal Pictures. He needed a new cartoon

   character for his own company. If Walt Disney

   _____ at Universal, he _____ his soon-to-be
   (stay) **(might / not create)**

   famous mouse along with artist Ub Iwerks.

3. Walt Disney's wife didn't like the name her husband chose for his new cartoon character.

   Mickey Mouse _____ as Mortimer Mouse if Disney's wife
   (could / end up)

   _____ with her husband's original idea for a name.
   (agree)

4. The first two Mickey Mouse cartoons had no sound. If Mickey _____
   (speak)

   in those short films, audiences _____ them more. As it was, they
   (might / enjoy)

   were not successful.

5. *Steamboat Willie* was the first Mickey Mouse cartoon with sound, and sound made all the

   difference. Mickey _____ a star by the end of 1928 if *Steamboat Willie*
   (not become)

   _____ music and sound effects.
   (not have)

6. From 1928 until 1946, Walt Disney's voice was the voice of Mickey Mouse. If Disney

   _____ someone else's voice to bring Mickey to life, the mouse
   (use)

   _____ so cute and charming, and fans _____
   (not be) **(might / not love)**

   him so much.

7. Walt Disney was a talented cartoonist, but he was also an intelligent businessman. Disney

_____ much less money if he _____ selling
          (make)   **(not start)**

toys, clothes, and other products when Mickey Mouse became popular.

8. After seeing the success of Mickey Mouse and the Walt Disney Company, the owners of

Universal Pictures probably wished that they _____ a way to keep
                                                              (find)

Disney at their company.

EXERCISE 2: Affirmative and Negative Statements

Complete the article about Walt Disney with the correct form of the verbs in parentheses.

Walt Disney had a difficult childhood, but he transformed his hardships into magic. Looking back, one can see the seeds of Disney's imagination in those early experiences. It's even possible that Disney ___wouldn't have created___ his many magical
                                                  1. (not create)
worlds if his early years _____ happier.
                                2. (be)

Disney's father, Elias Disney, had dreams too, but they never came true. After a business failure in Chicago, the Disneys moved to a farm in Missouri. If his two oldest brothers

_____ farmwork more enjoyable, Walt Disney's childhood
                   3. (find)

_____ easier. However, the oldest brothers soon returned to
                   4. (might / be)

Chicago, and six-year-old Walt and his brother Roy were left to do the farm chores. In an interesting parallel with the witch in *Snow White*, the Disneys sold apples door to door when they needed money. In time, Roy found jobs off the farm, and if Roy

_____ extra cash, Walt _____ never
               5. (not earn)

_____ a carnival or _____ a toy.
                6. (see)   **7. (own)**

Once, when Walt was seven, he painted large animals on the walls of the farmhouse. His father punished him severely, but others encouraged his talent. Some people believe that if

(continued on next page)

the local physician, "Doc" Sherwood, _____ him a quarter for a
8. (not pay)
drawing of his horse, Walt's life _____ a different outcome. And if his
9. (have)
Aunt Margaret _____ him a gift of drawing paper and crayons,
10. (not give)
Disney's genius _____ Elias's harsh treatment.
11. (not survive)

In 1910, when Walt was nine, Elias sold the farm and bought a newspaper route in Kansas

City, Missouri. For six years, Walt started work at 3:30 every morning. He sometimes fell

asleep in the warm halls of apartment buildings or dozed over a toy on a family's porch while

he was delivering newspapers. If he _____ more sleep during this
12. (get)
period, he _____ more attention to his lessons. But under the
13. (could / pay)
circumstances, he didn't have much success at school.

If he _____ Walter Pfeiffer, Disney's Kansas City boyhood
14. (not meet)
_____ completely joyless. Pfeiffer's family loved singing and telling
15. (might / be)
jokes, and they introduced Walt to vaudeville theater. "The Two Walts" even put together their

own show when they were thirteen. Disney's strict parents _____ if
16. (disapprove)
they _____ Walt was acting in vaudeville, so Walt used to sneak out
17. (know)
through his bedroom window to go to the theater to perform.

When Disney was fourteen, his father gave him permission to attend Saturday classes at the

Kansas City Art Institute. If Elias _____, Walt _____
18. (not agree) **19. (take)**
longer to find his vocation, but he was already dreaming of becoming a cartoonist. He

overcame great obstacles in his career, but once he had studied at the Institute, he never lost his

determination to make his imagined worlds real.

EXERCISE 3: Past Conditional with *Wish*

Toy Story is one of the most popular Disney movies. In the film, toys are alive, but only when humans aren't watching. The toys of a boy named Andy include Woody, who is a cowboy, and Buzz Lightyear, who thinks he's a real spaceman. Rewrite the sentences with **wish**.

1. **WOODY:** Buzz Lightyear took my place as Andy's favorite toy. Andy didn't get clothes and books for his birthday.

   I wish Buzz Lightyear hadn't taken

   my place as Andy's favorite toy.

   I wish Andy had gotten clothes and

   books for his birthday.

2. **MR. POTATO HEAD:** The kids didn't bring good presents to Andy's birthday party. There wasn't a Mrs. Potato Head toy in any of those boxes.

   _____

   _____

3. **REX:** Woody fought with Buzz. Buzz fell out the window.

   _____

   _____

4. **ANDY:** I lost Buzz Lightyear. I didn't have my favorite toy to take to Pizza Planet.

   _____

   _____

5. **BUZZ LIGHTYEAR:** I found out the truth about being a toy instead of a real spaceman. I wasn't able to save the universe from evil.

   _____

   _____

6. **WOODY AND BUZZ:** We didn't realize the importance of friendship. We didn't help each other sooner.

   _____

   _____

EXERCISE 4: Affirmative and Negative Statements

Using the words in parentheses, combine each pair of sentences into one past unreal conditional sentence. Keep the same order and decide which clause begins with **if.** *Make necessary changes in capitalization and punctuation.*

1. Disney lived on a farm. He drew wonderful cartoon animals. (might)

   If Disney hadn't lived on a farm, he might not have drawn wonderful cartoon animals.

2. He sold candy to train passengers as a boy. He loved model trains as an adult. (might)

   _____

   _____

3. He didn't join the army in World War I. He was too young. (would)

   _____

   _____

4. Disney met his fiancée's parents. His friend Ub gave him money to buy a suit. (could)

   _____

   _____

5. Disney needed the help of his brother Roy. He asked Roy to be his business partner. (would)

   _____

   _____

6. His art lessons meant a lot to Disney. He paid for lessons for Disney Studio artists. (would)

   _____

   _____

7. Disney made *Snow White and the Seven Dwarfs*. A bank loaned him $1.5 million. (could)

   _____

   _____

8. The movie succeeded. The bank didn't take Disney's home, his studio, and the film. (would)

   _____

   _____

9. Disney died in 1966. He didn't see the opening of the EPCOT Center in Florida. (would)

_____

_____

10. He overcame his unhappy childhood. He was a genius. (might)

_____

_____

EXERCISE 5: Questions and Responses

Complete the article with the correct form of the verbs in parentheses or with short answers.

The Second Time Around . . .

Our readers have shared some problems and questions related to their first trip to Disney World. First-time visitors can use their experiences and have more fun the first time around.

★ Orlando

Q: We visited Disney World for the first time last April, during spring break. It was packed! I think we spent most of our time waiting in lines. Is it always like that? _____ Would _____ we _____ have avoided _____ crowds if we
                 1. (avoid)
_____ had visited _____ at another time? —**Fred and Betty Ruddle, Flint, Michigan**
  2. (visit)
A: _____ Yes, you would have _____. Spring break is one of the most crowded times (along
     3.
with the Christmas holiday season and Presidents' Day weekend). Next time, go between

Thanksgiving and Christmas or between January 4 and the middle of February.

Q: We bought tickets to the park at our hotel (not a Disney hotel), and they were expensive.

How much _____ we _____ if we
              4. (save)
_____ them at a Disney hotel? —**K. Lewis, Denver, Colorado**
  5. (buy)
A: Up to 25 percent with a vacation package that included your hotel and entrance fees. But

remember that Disney hotels generally have a higher overall price.

(continued on next page)

Q: We visited Magic Kingdom first, and that was the end of the trip for our daughter—she never wanted to leave. She really couldn't appreciate EPCOT, which we visited next and which fascinated us. If you _____ the trip with a small child, where
6. (make)
_____ you _____ first? —**V. Luvik, Miami, Florida**
7. (go)

A: EPCOT. It's usually best to go there first, then MGM, and finally Magic Kingdom, which is fun for both adults and children.

Q: We stayed at a hotel inside the park because we wanted to be close to everything. Now we're wondering if we made the right choice. _____ we
_____ a long way if we _____ inside the park?
8. (travel)   9. (stay)
—**J. Méndez, San Juan, Puerto Rico**

A: _____. In fact, some of the hotels outside the park are
10.
actually closer to Magic Kingdom than some hotels inside the park, and rooms are definitely much cheaper.

Q: Our son was studying pirates at school, so our first day at Disney World we raced over to Pirates of the Caribbean. It was closed for repairs. If we _____
11. (call)
ahead, _____ they _____ us it was closed?
12. (tell)
—**P. James, Syracuse, New York**

A: _____. In fact, it's always a good idea to call, or even
13.
better, use the Disney website to find out if any rides are closed.

Q: On our first trip, we were never sure what to do next, and we spent a lot of time just waiting. My husband blamed the park, but I think we should have done things differently. If we _____ more, _____ we
14. (plan)
_____ our trip more? —**D. King, Dayton, Ohio**
15. (enjoy)
A: _____. There's so much to see that visitors can get
16.
overwhelmed. To get the best value for your money, plan each day ahead of time.

EXERCISE 6: Editing

Read Cassie's email to her sister. There are nine mistakes in the use of past unreal conditionals. The first mistake is already corrected. Find and correct eight more.

Dear Jenny,

    I just watched *Toy Story 3* on DVD. I really wish I had ~~see~~ *seen* the movie sooner. I knew it was the most popular movie of the summer in 2010, but I had no idea how good it really was. Honestly, if I would have known about the incredible animation in the film, I would have gone to a movie theater to see it. In fact, I would even have pay extra to see the 3D version. Yes, I know what you're thinking. You told me to see the film when it came out. I really wish I have listened to you.

    Luckily, I was able to download and watch *Toy Story* and *Toy Story 2*. I saw those movies a long time ago. If I hadn't watched them again, I might forgotten about Andy as a little boy and the relationships between Woody, Buzz Lightyear, and the other toys. It was interesting to see Andy as a college student in *Toy Story 3*. And Andy's mother played a small but important role again. The original *Toy Story* will never have happened if she hadn't given Buzz Lightyear to Andy as a birthday gift. In *Toy Story 3*, none of the important events would have occurred if she hadn't kept asking Andy to clean his room and if she didn't put Andy's toys in the garbage by mistake. Does Andy's mother remind you of anyone? We could had had a lot more free time as kids if Grandma weren't always forced us to pick up our toys, but she sure gave good presents!

    OK, that's all for now. You're still planning to go back home to visit Grandma next month, right? I'll see you then.

Cassie

EXERCISE 7: Personal Writing

Write a paragraph about one thing from your childhood that you wish had been different.
Use some of the phrases from the box.

I might not have . . .	If that had not occurred, . . .
I would have been . . . if . . .	Many people think about the past and wish . . .
If I had . . .	My childhood was great, but I wish . . .
If I had known . . .	My life would have been . . .

UNIT 25 Direct and Indirect Speech

EXERCISE 1: Direct and Indirect Speech

Circle the correct words to complete the report about lie-detector tests.

The Awful Truth

A number of years ago, the United States Supreme Court said / **told** private employers
1.
that you / they were no longer allowed to give lie-detector tests (also called polygraph tests)
2.
to people they wanted to hire. I was curious about these tests, so I decided to do a little bit

of research.

I talked to Erica Dale, who took a polygraph test when she began working in our

organization. She was one of the last employees to take one. "The examiner was very

nice," she told me. "He asked her / me a lot of harmless questions at first." During the test,
3.
Erica told the examiner that I / she lived in the suburbs. When he asked, she said that it
4.
was / is Monday and that she has taken / had taken the bus to my / her interview. Then he
5. **6.** **7.**
brought up some tougher subjects. "I told him / you that I got / 'd gotten into trouble for
8. **9.**
stealing in high school," Erica said. "I didn't try to justify my mistake, and there certainly

wasn't any point in lying about it."

Polygraphs are still given to employees of security firms and government agencies. They

are also used by the police. Nevertheless, many experts say that they didn't / don't measure
10.
truth—only physical reactions to questions. Some questions increase the average person's

blood pressure and create other physical changes that the polygraph measures, but do the

(continued on next page)

majority of tests give accurate results? "The tests <u>are / were</u> less than 50 percent accurate,"
11.
says one critic. "They simply do not reveal whether an individual is lying or telling the
truth."

Drew Faye, who served three years for a crime he didn't commit, agrees. After his arrest,
officials gave him a lie-detector test. They told him that <u>we / they</u> <u>plan / planned</u> to drop
12. **13.**
charges if <u>you / he</u> passed. "Hey, great," said Faye. Unfortunately, he failed—twice—and
14.
spent three years in jail. A few years later, someone <u>said / told</u> police that Faye actually
15.
<u>didn't commit / hadn't committed</u> the crime. Faye was released when the police learned the
16.
names of the real criminals.

A polygraph expert who saw the tests said that police <u>scored / had scored</u> Faye's tests
17.
improperly. Since his release, Faye has been campaigning against the use of polygraph tests.

EXERCISE 2: Direct and Indirect Speech: Necessary and Optional Tense Changes

Complete the interviewer's report of a job applicant's statements during a lie-detector test.
Change the verb tense for reported speech only when necessary.

The Applicant's Statements During the Test	The Interviewer's Report a Few Hours Later
1. "My name is Anita Bell."	She said _____*her name is Anita Bell.*_____
2. "It's Wednesday."	She said _____
3. "My husband drove me to the interview."	She stated _____
4. "Our house is near the lake."	She said _____
5. "I shoplifted a lipstick once as a teenager."	She admitted _____
6. "I went to my mother right away."	She added _____
7. "She took me to the store to return the lipstick."	She explained _____
8. "I always tell the truth."	She claimed _____
9. "The test seems easy."	She said _____
10. "I don't mind taking lie-detector tests."	She noted _____

EXERCISE 3: Direct and Indirect Speech

Compare the statements from a job interview with the previous employer's information form. Use **say** *or* **tell** *to report the statements. Then write* **That's true** *or* **That's not true.**

BATES DEPARTMENT STORE
EMPLOYEE INFORMATION FORM

Name:	Ethan Taylor
Dates employed:	Feb. 2007–Jan. 2010
Position (start):	Salesclerk
Promotions?	No
How many employees did this employee supervise?	None
Salary:	Start: $20,500 per year
	Finish: $22,000
Supervisor's comments:	This employee performed well on the job. He was reliable, and he showed initiative in serving customers and keeping the department running smoothly.
Reason for leaving:	Laid off when the store reduced its staff
Eligible for rehire:	Yes

1. "My name is Ethan Taylor."

   He said his name is Ethan Taylor. That's true.

2. "I worked at Bates Department Store for four years."

   He told the interviewer that he'd worked at Bates Department Store for four years.

   That's not true.

3. "I was a salesclerk."

   _____

   _____

4. "Then I received a promotion to supervisor."

   _____

   _____

5. "I supervised five other salesclerks."

   _____

   _____

(continued on next page)

6. "I was a reliable employee."

_____

_____

7. "I showed initiative."

_____

_____

8. "My employers liked my work."

_____

_____

9. "Bates didn't fire me."

_____

_____

10. "I lost my job because of staff reductions."

_____

_____

11. "I earned $25,000 a year."

_____

_____

12. "I got a raise of more than $2,000."

_____

_____

EXERCISE 4: Editing

Read the journal entries. There are nine mistakes in the use of direct and indirect speech.
The first mistake is already corrected. Find and correct eight more.

November 7

                                                         'd lost

I called Jason last week and told him that I ~~'ve lost~~ my job. Jason was such

a good friend that he offered to lend me some money, but I explained that I had saved enough to be prepared in case of an emergency. I was hoping for a job at his father's company, but Jason said me that he wasn't aware of any available positions.

November 8

Everyone says that it was difficult to get a job these days, but Rachel says that she'd always believed in me. She's my biggest supporter. She keeps telling me that you have a great chance of finding a job soon.

November 9

I went to a job placement agency this morning to meet with a recruiter. The recruiter told that she wants to give me a computer skills test. After I finished the test, she said that she was very pleased with your score on the test. In fact, she said, "I know of several jobs that you're qualified for."

November 15

The recruiter has been very helpful. I had an interview this afternoon. It went well. The manager told me that I was my last appointment of the day. Maybe that means I'll be the first person that he thinks of when he makes his final decision. I hope so!

EXERCISE 5: Personal Writing

On a separate piece of paper, write a paragraph about a lie that later caused problems for you. Use some of the phrases from the box.

After people found out, . . .	I told . . .
I lied because . . .	If I were in the same situation again, I . . .
I made a serious mistake when I said . . .	Later, I said . . .
I really wish . . .	The problem occurred when . . .

EXERCISE 1: Direct and Indirect Speech

*In January 1994, there was a terrible earthquake in Los Angeles, California. Read what John Baker said about it in 1994. Then use **He said** with indirect speech to write what a friend in New York reported a year later.*

1. "I am living in Los Angeles."

   He said that he was living in Los Angeles.

2. "I've been living here my whole life."

   _____

3. "I've experienced many earthquakes in my years here."

   _____

4. "This quake was the worst."

   _____

5. "I'll start to repair the damage on my house this week."

   _____

6. "I must stay optimistic."

   _____

7. "I may get government aid next month to restore my one-hundred-year-old home."

   _____

8. "I can't afford earthquake insurance right now."

   _____

9. "I had looked into it before the earthquake."

   _____

10. "I should have bought some insurance then."

    _____

EXERCISE 2: Direct and Indirect Speech

Read what people in Los Angeles said about the 1994 quake. Use **He said** *or* **She said** *to report the people's statements.*

1. "I was never so afraid in my life." —*Miriam Shakter, human resources manager*

   <u>She said that she'd never been so afraid in her life.</u>

2. "I felt a sensation of falling." —*Diane Stillman, paralegal*

   _____

3. "We were all pretty well prepared for an earthquake, but not for the fire." —*Al McNeill, Los Angeles resident*

   _____

4. "The walls of these buildings may collapse at any time." —*unidentified fireman*

   _____

5. "I haven't seen anything like it." —*Robert DeFeo, Chief of the Fire Department*

   _____

6. "It felt like a giant hand reaching down and shaking me." —*Seventy-three-year-old man*

   _____

7. "I'm scared that there's going to be another one." —*Eight-year-old girl*

   _____

8. "I'm so glad I'm here!" —*Andrea Donnellan, geophysicist*

   _____

9. "Although I've been through war in my country, I had no idea what to do in the quake." —*Nicaraguan woman*

   _____

   _____

10. "If my house can't be saved, I don't know how I'll bear it because I'll have no place to live." —*Eighty-six-year-old woman*

    _____

    _____

A. *Read the interview between* Today's World (TW) *and geophysicist Dr. M. T. Ito* (ITO).

When the Earth Moves

An Interview with Geophysicist M. T. Ito

TW: *Was the Los Angeles quake the worst in California's history?*

ITO: Not at all. The San Francisco quake of 1906 was much worse.

TW: *Earthquakes aren't very common, are they?*

ITO: Actually, there could be as many as a million earthquakes a year.

TW: *A million a year!*

ITO: Yes. Several thousand of them may occur today. However, most will go unnoticed because they'll occur beneath the ocean surface.

TW: *But even those earthquakes can be dangerous.*

ITO: You're right. Some have started dangerous tidal waves. We all remember, for example, the terrible tsunami in December 2004 that occurred following an earthquake under the Indian Ocean. The tsunami killed hundreds of thousands of people. And there was the earthquake and tsunami that hit Japan in March 2011, causing what might be the worst nuclear accident in history.

TW: *What causes earthquakes?*

ITO: I can't explain in great detail because it would be too complicated. Basically, quakes happen as a result of sudden movement in the rocks below the Earth's surface. Forces push against the rocks, and the rocks break along lines called *faults*. In fact, a hidden fault caused the January 1994 Los Angeles quake.

TW: *Southern California gets more than its fair share of quakes, doesn't it?*

ITO: Yes. It has had several strong quakes in the past 20 years.

TW: *Can't scientists predict them?*

ITO: Another interviewer just asked me this very same question yesterday. As I explained to him, scientists may be able to make more accurate predictions sometime in the future. At present, they can tell you where an earthquake will occur, but not when.

TW: *That's really terrible. Isn't there anything we can do?*

ITO: Yes. Engineers have developed houses and other structures that are able to withstand earthquake shocks. Governments must enforce building requirements in earthquake zones to limit damage from earthquakes.

TW: *What can individual citizens do?*

ITO: People living in earthquake zones should always be prepared because a quake might occur at any time. It's a good idea for them to have an emergency plan and emergency equipment, such as a first-aid kit, a battery-powered radio, a flashlight, and extra batteries.

B. *Read the statements about Dr. Ito's interview. For each statement, write* **That's right** *or* **That's wrong** *and use the verb in parentheses to report what Dr. Ito said.*

1. The 1994 Los Angeles quake wasn't as bad as the quake that hit San Francisco in 1906.

   (said) *That's right. She said that the San Francisco quake of 1906 had been much worse.*

2. Earthquakes aren't common.

   (explain) *That's wrong. She explained that there could be as many as a million*

   earthquakes a year.

3. It's possible that there were earthquakes on the day of Dr. Ito's interview.

   (say) _____

   _____

4. Most quakes take place under water.

   (say) _____

   _____

5. Earthquakes beneath the ocean are not dangerous.

   (acknowledge) _____

   _____

6. There were a lot of people who died in the 2004 tsunami in the Indian Ocean.

   (add) _____

   _____

7. It's easy to explain the cause of earthquakes.

   (state) _____

   _____

8. A visible fault caused the 1994 Los Angeles quake.

   (indicate) _____

   _____

(continued on next page)

9 Southern California gets a lot of quakes.

(note) _____

_____

10. Another interviewer wanted to know about scientists' ability to predict earthquakes.

(say) _____

_____

11. Scientists will never be able to predict earthquakes accurately.

(claim) _____

_____

12. People living in earthquake zones can do something to be prepared.

(say) _____

_____

EXERCISE 4: Editing

Read the article. There are eight mistakes in the use of direct and indirect speech. The first mistake is already corrected. Find and correct seven more.

Real-Life Geography

News reports about the tsunami in the Indian Ocean on December 26, 2004, said that
                          had been able to
children ~~are able to~~ save lives that day. In a recent interview, Dr. M. T. Ito explained why. She

observed that the children have remembered their geography lessons that day.

Dr. Ito pointed out that tourists on the beaches in places like Thailand were amazed when

the water of the Indian Ocean receded at the start of the tsunami. As the water pulled back,

they followed it so that they could see the unusual sight. Dr. Ito said that many of the tourists

are taking photos instead of evacuating the beach. However, there were others, including

children, who understood the danger. Because they knew about geography, they quickly

explained that a powerful wave of water will return in about five minutes. They told their family and friends that they have to leave the beach and go to higher ground right now. And once

they were in a safe place, they told everyone they should stay here because one large wave did

not mean that the tsunami is over.

In the words of Dr. Ito, "You can never know too much about Earth science." So if you're a

student, pay attention in geography class. If you're not, it might be a good idea to watch the

National Geographic Channel on TV.

EXERCISE 5: Personal Writing

*Write a paragraph to retell a story that you heard on the news about a flood, an earthquake,
or another disaster. Use some of the phrases from the box.*

Another pointed out . . .	People who were interviewed stated . . .
At the end of the news report, I said . . .	The most recent reports say that the situation . . .
I felt . . . when I heard . . .	The reporter added . . .
It occurred . . .	The reporter announced . . .
One person explained . . .	The reporter didn't say . . .

Indirect Instructions, Commands, Requests, and Invitations

EXERCISE 1: Direct and Indirect Speech

Write sentences in direct and indirect speech. Choose between **She told me** *and* **She asked me** *for the sentences in indirect speech.*

1. (direct speech)   "Turn left."

   (indirect speech)   *She told me to turn left.*

2. (direct speech)   "Don't turn right."

   (indirect speech)   _____

3. (direct speech)   _____

   (indirect speech)   She told me to slow down.

4. (direct speech)   _____

   (indirect speech)   She told me not to drive so fast.

5. (direct speech)   "Can you please turn on the radio?"

   (indirect speech)   _____

6. (direct speech)   _____

   (indirect speech)   She asked me to open the window.

7. (direct speech)   _____

   (indirect speech)   She asked me to come in for coffee.

8. (direct speech)   "Don't park in the bus stop."

   (indirect speech)   _____

Read the travel tips about the common and very dangerous problem of feeling sleepy when driving from SafeCarTravel.com.

Tips for Staying Awake While Driving

1. Get enough sleep before beginning a long trip.

2. Eat something before leaving on a trip.

3. Don't rely on caffeinated beverages, such as coffee or cola, to stay awake.

4. Share the driving responsibilities with another person if possible to avoid fatigue.

5. Don't wait until you're sleepy to take a break.

6. Stop every couple of hours and stretch your legs by walking around.

7. Listen to music or a book on tape as a remedy for sleepiness.

8. Don't allow daydreaming to interfere with driving.

9. Don't park on the side of the road if you need to stop for a short nap.

Complete the sentences, rewriting the advice in indirect speech.

1. SafeCarTravel.com tells _drivers to get enough sleep before beginning a long trip._

2. The website tells _drivers to eat something before leaving on a trip._

3. It also warns _____

4. The site tells _____

5. It tells _____

6. It urges _____

7. It advises _____

8. It cautions _____

9. It warns _____

Circle the correct words to complete the journal entry.

Last Friday, my neighbor called me. She (invited) / told me to go
1.
for a ride in her new car. I told her I would love to. As soon as I
got into the car, she told / invited me to buckle my seat belt. I was
2.
pleased because I thought this meant she was a safe driver. Was I
wrong! The experience was absolutely astonishing. I watched as the
speedometer approached and then passed 80 mph. I told her
slow / to slow down. I begged her not to / to not speed.
3.   **4.**
She slowed down for a while, but then she sped up again.
Suddenly we heard a siren. The police officer told her pull / to pull
5.
over and stop. He got out of the car and asked her
to show / not to show him her license. She only had a learner's
6.
permit! He advised / ordered her to give him the permit, and, after
7.
checking my license, he told me that to take / to take the wheel and
8.
follow him to the police station. Two hours later, on the way home
from the station, my neighbor invited / ordered me to have dinner
9.
at her place. She had just bought a new microwave oven that she
wanted to try out. I thanked her but asked her waiting / to wait
10.
until another day. I had a headache and needed to take a nap!

Reread the story in Exercise 3. Then rewrite the indirect speech as direct speech. The numbers in the art match the numbers in Exercise 3.

1. Would you like to go for a ride in my new car?

Read the journal entry. There are eight mistakes in the use of direct and indirect speech.
The first mistake is already corrected. Find and correct seven more.

                                                                        to

     My neighbor Jeanette is still a terrible driver. I advised her ^ go to driving school, but her first lesson was bad, really bad. To start with, she was drinking a large cup of hot coffee when she got in the car. The driving instructor told her that to throw the coffee away. He ordered her no to have any food or drink in the vehicle during a lesson. When she turned the volume on the radio way up and began singing along with her favorite rock music, he said turn the radio off. Then, just as the instructor was warning her to paid attention, her cell phone rang and she answered it. I can only imagine how angry he was, but of course Jeanette didn't think it was a problem. She was actually surprised that the instructor told her to get out of the car.

     When Jeanette told me the story, I couldn't stop laughing—until she asked me to be her driving teacher. I mean, look at what happened the last time I got in the car with her! I said that I wouldn't give her lessons, but I agreed to call the driving school for her. I asked the instructor giving her a second chance. He agreed, but only if Jeanette promised to do everything that he said. He said that he would monitor her progress closely and added that if Jeanette's problems persisted, he would tell her leave again. I cautioned Jeanette not to cause any more problems.

     Jeanette has been lucky so far. She got her learner's permit back after that horrible night at the police station, and she might still finish driving school and get her license. And if she does get a driver's license, I know one thing for sure. I'll be the one who drives if she invites me to going out with her.

Write a paragraph to tell a story about a time that you did not do what you were told to do.
Use some of the phrases from the box.

. . . warned me . . . , but . . .	I got in trouble because . . .
Although . . . ordered me . . .	I learned an important lesson. I now know . . .
I did not . . . because . . .	In the future, when I am told . . .
I finally . . .	When . . . told me . . . , I . . .

UNIT 28 Indirect Questions

EXERCISE 1: Word Order

Lydia Chan interviewed her grandmother for a family-history project at school. The next day, her grandmother told a friend about their talk. Put the words in parentheses into the correct order and write Lydia's questions as her grandmother reported them.

1. "Can I talk to you about your life?"

   She asked if she could talk to me about my life.
   (about my life / if / could / she / talk to me)

2. "Do you have time today?"

   _____
   (whether / had / I / time / yesterday)

3. "Could you show me some photos?"

   _____
   (could / I / if / show her some photos)

4. "What's your full name?"

   _____
   (was / my full name / what)

5. "Who chose your name?"

   _____
   (who / my name / had chosen)

6. "When were you born?"

   _____
   (born / I / when / was)

7. "What country did your family come from?"

   _____
   (my family / what country / had come from)

8. "Where were you born?"

   _____
   (where / I / born / was)

9. "What was your biggest adventure?"

   _____
   (my biggest adventure / had been / what)

10. "What are you most proud of?"

   _____
   (was / I / what / most proud of)

Complete the article by changing the direct questions in parentheses to indirect questions.

BRINGING HISTORY HOME

by Monica Lubecki

A poor young man who had just arrived in the United States saw a fruit vendor on a New York street. He pointed at a piece of fruit and paid for it. But he didn't ask _____*what it was*_____. He bit into what he
1. (What is it?)
thought was an orange and quickly spit it out. It was a bitter kumquat—and he had spent precious money on it!

The young man was my grandfather. My mother told the story countless times, always with the same sad little smile. I loved hearing it and often interrupted with questions to prolong it. For example, I always asked

_____. "Nineteen," she reported. Then I
2. (How old was he?)
asked _____. "Five cents." Finally, I
3. (How much did it cost?)
demanded to know _____. She always
4. (Why didn't he ask the name of the fruit?)
replied impatiently, "You know he couldn't speak English."

As an adult, I asked myself _____. Later,
5. (Why did the details seem so important?)
I learned that our story was a typical immigrant family story. Children in a family trying to handle the pressure of living in a new country couldn't ask

_____, so the family told a story that
6. (How are we going to get by?)
explained the methods they used to survive. (Our family's favorite rule was "Ask questions!")

(continued on next page)

Everyone has good stories, and collecting them is an interesting way for younger family members to stay close to older relatives and learn the family's culture. However, there are potential problems when it comes to asking appropriate questions and making the older family members feel comfortable with a family history project. Recently, my son Mark interviewed his grandfather, my husband's father. If you'd like to try this in your family, here are the steps Mark took to make his grandfather feel at ease.

1. Mark asked him politely _____.
   7. (Do you have some time to talk to me?)
2. He found a quiet room to talk in and then asked his grandfather

   _____.
   8. (Do you feel comfortable here?)
3. To get started, Mark talked about an event that the two of them had once

   shared. He asked his grandfather _____.
   9. (Do you remember our trip to the circus?)

When the interview got under way, Mark wanted to know about the details of his

grandfather's childhood. He asked him _____ and
10. (What did you wear to school?)

_____. In addition, he asked his grandfather
11. (What did your mother cook?)

_____. A little later, when Mark asked him
12. (What hobbies did you have?)

_____, he learned how his hobby, amateur radio, led
13. (What was your most important decision?)

to his job in communications. At the end of the interview, when he asked his grandfather

_____, he learned about his fascination with
14. (What new invention do you like best?)

computers.

In this interview, Mark discovered things that we, his parents, had never known about

our own parents' generation and ideas.

A reporter interviewed Maya Angelou, an American poet who has led a very interesting life. Read the interviewer's notes and report which of his questions he asked and which ones he didn't ask.

1. when/born?
2. who/gave the nickname Maya?   brother Bailey (called her "Mine")
3. where/grew up?   St. Louis and San Francisco
4. why/moved to San Francisco?
5. what/studied?   dance and drama in a special high school
6. worked during high school?   yes—streetcar conductor, cook, singer, dancer
7. ever lived in another country?   yes—in Egypt—with husband, a lawyer from South Africa
8. speak other languages?   yes—fluent in French, Spanish, Italian, Arabic, and Fanti
9. why/name first book
    I Know Why the Caged Bird Sings?
10. why/started writing?   inspired by a speech by Dr. Martin Luther King, Jr.
11. studied writing in school?
12. how/evaluate your own work?

1. He didn't ask her when she was born.

2. He asked her who had given her the nickname Maya.

3. _____

4. _____

5. _____

6. _____

7. _____

8. _____

9. _____

10. _____

11. _____

12. _____

EXERCISE 4: Editing

Read the opening paragraph of a student research paper. There are seven mistakes in the use of direct and indirect speech. The first mistake is already corrected. Find and correct six more.

After I saw the movie *Invictus*, I wanted to know more about it, so I watched several interviews with the film's director, Clint Eastwood. In each case, the interviewers asked why ~~had Eastwood decided~~ *Eastwood had decided* to make a movie about the 1995 South African team that won the Rugby World Cup championship. They asked how much you liked sports, and they tried to find out whether the 2009 movie had a connection with the 2010 World Cup soccer tournament in South Africa. Several interviewers wanted to know if was Eastwood's interest in politics part of his decision to make the film? They also asked how much did the movie cost, especially since much of it was shot in South Africa. No one had to ask who was Nelson Mandela, but many wanted to know when the former South African president had come up with the idea of using a rugby championship to handle political problems. That was exactly the kind of question I became interested in. Because I am a sports fan, I originally wanted to learn more about the South African rugby team, the Springboks, and their captain, François Pienaar. However, I soon began to ask how Mandela could go from prisoner to presidential candidate to world leader to Nobel Prize winner? This paper will report the results of my research. It will focus on the reasons that Nelson Mandela won the 1993 Nobel Peace Prize.

EXERCISE 5: Personal Writing

Find out about an interesting family story by interviewing a member of your family or by interviewing a friend about his or her family. Then write one or two paragraphs about the story on a separate piece of paper. Use some of the phrases from the box.

. . . explained that . . .	I got a very interesting answer when I asked . . .
. . . told me that . . .	I talked to . . . because . . .
First, I asked . . .	I wanted to know . . .
From this story, I learned . . .	Next, I wanted to find out . . . , so . . .

EXERCISE 1: Embedded Questions: Word Order and Punctuation

Complete the conversation by changing the direct questions in parentheses to embedded questions. Use correct punctuation.

A: Do you know *if there is anything good on TV?*
                      1. (Is there anything good on TV?)

B: There's a soccer game on this evening that I want to watch.

A: I don't understand _____
                      2. (Why do you enjoy watching sports all the time?)

B: Well, I want to know _____
                      3. (How can you watch those boring travel shows?)

A: I like to find out _____
                      4. (What are the ultimate travel destinations?)

B: But you never go anywhere. Can you remember _____
                      5. (When was your last vacation?)

A: That's beside the point. I'm not sure _____
                      6. (Am I going to take a vacation anytime soon?)

It depends on my work and school schedules. But I can dream, can't I?

B: OK. Can you explain _____
                      7. (How are you going to pay for your dream vacation?)

A: I'm trying to figure out _____
                      8. (How much will a volunteer vacation cost?)

B: I've always wondered _____
                      9. (Do people really take vacations where they have to work?)

A: Of course they do. Volunteer vacations are becoming more and more popular. They're a great way to travel. They're not too expensive, and they give people a chance to see the world and help others at the same time.

B: Do you know _____
                      10. (Which organization has volunteer vacations in Africa?)

A: The one that I've heard the most about is Global Volunteers, but there are other groups that arrange trips too.

B: Could you tell me _____
                      11. (Where should I go for more information?)

A: The Internet is a good place to go—or you could try watching a few travel shows with me!

A. *Look at the list of questions that students in a listening-speaking class prepared for Jake Davis, a guest speaker who was invited to their class to talk about volunteer vacations.*

Questions for Mr. Davis

~~Why do students take volunteer vacations?~~

What is the average cost of a volunteer vacation?

Who pays for the trip?

When do most students take volunteer vacations?

How long do the trips ordinarily last?

Will I have any free time on a volunteer vacation?

How far in advance do I have to plan a volunteer vacation?

Do I have to be over 21 to go on a volunteer vacation?

Are most of the volunteer opportunities in the U.S.?

Should students on a volunteer vacation bring any extra money?

B. *Complete the conversation that took place during the students' question-and-answer session with Mr. Davis. Choose the appropriate question from the list, and change it to an embedded question. Use correct punctuation.*

1. **KHADIJA:** I'm not sure ___why students take volunteer vacations.___
    Isn't the whole point of a vacation to relax and have fun?

    MR. DAVIS: A volunteer vacation is totally logical. Many students like the idea of traveling and doing service work. They can do something useful while they're experiencing the customs of a different culture, learning new ideas, and, yes, even having fun.

2. **VICKY:** I'm only eighteen, so I'd like to know _____

    MR. DAVIS: There are volunteer vacations for people of all ages, but you may need your parents' permission for some of them since you're not twenty-one.

3. **JIN HO:** Can you tell me _____

    MR. DAVIS: The individual traveler pays.

4. **NIDA:** Could you clarify _____

MR. DAVIS: The cost depends on the location, the length, and the type of trip. The price can be anywhere from several hundred to several thousand dollars.

5. **MACHIKO:** Do you know _____

MR. DAVIS: It's always a good idea to have money for emergencies or something that you really want to buy as a souvenir.

6. **BILL:** I'd like to find out _____

MR. DAVIS: You'll spend most of your time on a volunteer project, but you'll still have a chance to meet the local people and have cultural experiences on your own.

7. **GOSHA:** Can you tell me _____

MR. DAVIS: The majority of the trips are from one to three weeks.

8. **KHADIJA:** I'm wondering _____

MR. DAVIS: Some travel during the summer, but others do a volunteer vacation when they have a semester break.

9. **NIDA:** Do you know _____

MR. DAVIS: Some are in the U.S., but there are volunteer opportunities in countries all around the world.

10. **KE:** I have a travel brochure about volunteer vacations, but it doesn't actually say

_____

MR. DAVIS: I suggest making your travel plans as soon as possible. That way, you'll be sure to get the trip that you want.

EXERCISE 3: Infinitives After Question Words

Read the conversation about traveling. Then use the correct question word and the infinitive form of the appropriate verbs to complete the summaries.

1. **SYLVIA:** There are several airlines that fly from Chicago to Madrid. I have no idea which one I should take.

SUMMARY: Sylvia is trying to figure out _which airline to take._

2. **ANNE:** Look for a nonstop flight and the lowest possible airfare.

SYLVIA: Where?

ANNE: I usually go to a website like Orbitz or Travelocity.

SUMMARY: Sylvia isn't sure _____

(continued on next page)

3.   **Sylvia:** OK. I'm thinking about renting a car. My question is how.

     Anne: It's cheaper if you rent a car before you leave. You can do that on Orbitz or

     Travelocity too.

   summary: Sylvia and Anne are discussing _____

4.   **Sylvia:** That was easy enough.

     Anne: What are you going to do about rental car insurance?

     Sylvia: Oh, you're right. I'd better talk to my agent.

   summary: Sylvia will ask her insurance agent _____

5.   **Anne:** Do you speak Spanish?

     Sylvia: A little, and I know where I can go for an inexpensive language course.

   summary: Sylvia has already found out _____

6.   **Anne:** How long are you going to stay in Spain?

     Sylvia: Maybe two weeks—or maybe longer.

   summary: Sylvia can't decide _____

7.   **Anne:** What kind of clothes are you going to pack?

     Sylvia: I've been thinking about that a lot.

   summary: Sylvia is wondering _____

8.   **Anne:** Is there someone you can talk to about hotels and restaurants?

     Sylvia: I can't think of anyone.

   summary: Sylvia doesn't know _____

Read the email. There are six mistakes in the use of embedded questions. The first mistake is already corrected. Find and correct five more. Don't forget to check punctuation.

Dear Alicia,

    I don't know when ~~are you~~ *you're* leaving for your trip, but I decided to write anyway. How are you? Dan and I and the kids are all fine. Busy as usual. Tonight Dan and I got a babysitter and went to the movies (we hardly ever have the chance to go out alone). We saw a romantic comedy called *The Wedding Date*. I don't know is it playing near you, but I recommend it.

    I was thinking about the last time we were in San Francisco together. Can you remember where we ate. I know the restaurant was somewhere in Chinatown, but I can't remember what it was called.

    I've been wondering why I haven't heard from Wu-lan? Do you know where did he move? I'd like to write to him, but I don't know how to contact him.

    Well, the summer is almost here. Let us know when can you come for a visit. It would be great to see you again.

All my best,

Lily

EXERCISE 5: Personal Writing

Write a paragraph about a volunteer opportunity in your school or in the place where you live. Write about the questions you have about the volunteer work. Use some of the phrases from the box.

Before I volunteer, I need to find out how . . .

I don't know whether or not . . .

I hope that there is someone who can . . .

I will decide . . .

I wonder if . . .

I would really like to know . . .

I'm interested in doing volunteer work at . . .

The volunteer work sounds interesting, but I don't understand . . .

WORKBOOK ANSWER KEY

In this answer key, where the short or contracted form is given, the full or long form is also correct and where the full form is given, the contracted form is often also correct.

UNIT 1 (pages 1–4)

EXERCISE 1

2. ask, asking
3. buys, buying
4. come, comes
5. do, doing
6. eats, eating
7. employ, employs
8. fly, flies
9. forgets, forgetting
10. have, having
11. hurries, hurrying
12. lie, lies
13. opens, opening
14. rains, raining
15. reaches, reaching
16. say, saying
17. ties, tying
18. control, controls

EXERCISE 2

A. 2. Are . . . taking
3. is studying
4. 's
5. remember
6. look

B. 1. Do . . . know
2. teaches
3. 's working
4. does . . . mean
5. don't believe

C. 1. do . . . spell
2. have
3. looks

D. 1. are . . . sitting
2. don't seem
3. 'm trying
4. doesn't like
5. writes
6. is
7. 's beginning

E. 1. Do . . . want
2. is studying
3. does . . . do
4. analyzes
5. write
6. sign

EXERCISE 3

2. doesn't know
3. is focusing
4. is writing
5. looks
6. studies
7. believe
8. gives
9. are using OR use
10. convinces
11. does . . . hope OR is . . . hoping
12. look
13. tells
14. Does . . . lean
15. indicates
16. represents
17. is planning
18. doesn't leave OR didn't leave
19. doesn't avoid
20. show
21. 's
22. is investigating
23. thinks
24. takes
25. warns
26. doesn't guarantee

EXERCISE 4

Well, I'm here at my new school, and ~~I'm liking~~ *I like* it very much. I'm ~~study~~ *studying* in the English Institute this semester, and the style of the classes is really different from our English classes in Korea. My teachers ~~doesn't~~ *don't* know how to speak Korean, and my classmates ~~are coming~~ *come* from countries all around the world, so we use English all the time. That ~~is meaning~~ *means* that I'm getting a lot of good practice these days.

Although I'm very happy, sometimes ~~I'm having~~ *I have* problems. ~~I'm not~~ *I don't* understand my classmates' names because they don't look or sound like Korean names. I always ask the same questions: "What's your name?" and "How *do* you spell it?" I want to use names with titles like "Mr. Hoffman" and "Prof. Li" for my teachers, but they want me to call them by their first names. It's difficult for me to treat my teachers so informally, but I *'m* trying. Slowly but surely, I'm getting accustomed to my life here.

I miss you a lot. ~~You~~ *You're* still my favorite English teacher.

EXERCISE 5

Answers will vary.

UNIT 2 (pages 5–9)

EXERCISE 1

2. apply
3. was, were
4. became
5. carried
6. developed
7. eat
8. fell
9. feel
10. got
11. grew
12. lived
13. meet
14. pay
15. permitted
16. planned
17. send
18. slept

EXERCISE 2

2. met
3. asked
4. Was
5. did . . . notice
6. Were . . . going
7. found
8. didn't fall
9. were working
10. met
11. hired
12. was trying
13. was
14. was feeling OR felt
15. was pretending OR
   pretended
16. thought
17. wanted
18. was working
19. came
20. didn't ask
21. solved
22. stopped
23. fell
24. were taking
25. met
26. became
27. was dating
28. didn't seem
29. heard
30. was whispering
31. got
32. told
33. wanted
34. changed
35. realized
36. didn't stop
37. broke up
38. asked
39. was moving
40. saw
41. was sitting
42. was trying
43. jumped
44. thought
45. didn't ask
46. was helping
47. seemed
48. saw
49. introduced
50. invited

EXERCISE 3

2. While he was drinking a glass of water, he broke the glass. OR He was drinking a glass of water when he broke the glass.
3. When he stood up to greet Dana, he fell on the wet floor.
4. He forgot Dana's name when he wanted to introduce her to a friend.
5. While he was eating a plate of spaghetti, he got some sauce on Dana's dress. OR He was eating a plate of spaghetti when he got some sauce on Dana's dress.
6. He had no money when he got the check at the end of dinner.
7. He was thinking only about Dana while he was driving home. OR While he was driving home, he was thinking only about Dana.
8. When he received a phone call from Dana, he was recovering from his car accident. OR He received a phone call from Dana while he was recovering from his car accident.

EXERCISE 4

I'm really glad that I ~~was deciding~~ *decided* to rent this apartment. I almost ~~wasn't~~ *didn't* move here because the rent is a little high, but I'm happy to be here. All the other apartments I researched ~~were seeming~~ *seemed* too small, and the neighborhoods just weren't as beautiful as this one. And moving wasn't as bad as I feared. My original plan was to take a week off from work, but when Hakim ~~was offering~~ *offered* to help, I didn't need so much time. What a great brother! We ~~were moving~~ *moved* everything into the apartment in two days. The man next door was really nice to us. On the second day, he even helped Hakim with some of the heavy furniture. His name is Jared. I ~~don't~~ *didn't* even unpack the kitchen stuff last weekend because I was so tired. Last night I ~~walking~~ *walked* Mitzi for only two blocks. When I came back, Jared ~~stood~~ *was standing* downstairs. I think I made him nervous because he ~~was dropping~~ *dropped* his mail when he saw me. When he recovered, we talked for a few minutes. I'd like to ask him over for coffee this weekend (in order to thank him), but everything is still in boxes. Maybe in a couple of weeks . . .

EXERCISE 5

Answers will vary.

UNIT 3 (pages 10–16)

EXERCISE 1

2. brought, brought
3. chose, chosen
4. delayed, delayed
5. felt, felt
6. found, found
7. finished, finished
8. got, gotten
9. graduated, graduated
10. hid, hidden
11. noticed, noticed
12. omitted, omitted
13. owned, owned
14. read, read
15. replied, replied
16. ripped, ripped
17. showed, shown
18. spoke, spoken

EXERCISE 2

2. She graduated from college in 2005.
3. She's been reporting OR She's reported crime news since 2008.
4. Recently, she's been researching crime in schools.
5. She's been working on her master's degree since 2008.
6. Her father worked for the Broadfield Police Department for 20 years.
7. Simon Pohlig moved to Broadfield in 2006.
8. He's owned the historic Sharney's Restaurant since 2008.

9. A friend introduced Simon and Nakisha at the restaurant one night.
10. He coached basketball for the Boys and Girls Club for two years.
11. He's written two cookbooks for children.
12. He's been planning a local television show since January of this year.
13. Nakisha and Simon have been engaged for one year.

EXERCISE 3

2. applied
3. has been working OR has worked
4. has written
5. found, was
6. has attended
7. began, received
8. went on
9. has taken
10. started
11. didn't get
12. decided
13. hasn't received
14. lived
15. has lived OR has been living
16. has recommended OR recommended
17. left
18. hasn't told
19. didn't slant
20. explained

EXERCISE 4

My grandson and his girlfriend have ~~made~~ *been making* wedding plans for the past few months. At first I was delighted, but last week I ~~have heard~~ *heard* something that changed my feelings. It seems that our future granddaughter-in-law has ~~been deciding~~ *decided* to keep her own last name after the wedding. Her reasons: First, she doesn't want to "lose her identity." Her parents ~~have named~~ *named* her 31 years ago, and she ~~was~~ *has been* Donna Esposito since then. She sees no reason to change now. Second, she is a member of the Rockland Symphony Orchestra and she ~~performed~~ *has performed* OR *has been performing* with them for eight years. As a result, she ~~already became~~ *has already become* known professionally by her maiden name.

John, when I~~'ve gotten~~ *got* married, I didn't think of keeping my maiden name. I ~~have felt~~ *felt* so proud when I became "Mrs. Smith." We named our son after my father, but our surname showed that we three were a family.

I've ~~been reading~~ *read* two articles on this topic, and I can now understand her decision to use her maiden name professionally. But I still can't understand why she wants to use it socially.

My husband and I ~~tried~~ *have tried* many times to hide our hurt feelings, but it's been getting harder. I want to tell her and my grandson what I think, but I don't want to ruin his wedding celebration.

My grandson ~~didn't say~~ *hasn't said* anything so far, so we don't know how he feels. ~~Have we been making~~ *Have we made* the right choice by keeping quiet?

A Concerned Grandmother Who ~~Hasn't Been Saying~~ *Hasn't Said* One Word Yet

EXERCISE 5

Answers will vary.

UNIT 4 (pages 17–25)

EXERCISE 1

2. break, broken
3. cutting, cut
4. doing, done
5. entertaining, entertained
6. fight, fighting
7. forgiving, forgiven
8. lead, led
9. planning, planned
10. practicing, practiced
11. quitting, quit
12. seek, seeking
13. sink, sinking
14. stealing, stolen
15. sweeping, swept
16. swimming, swum
17. tell, told
18. withdraw, withdrawing

EXERCISE 2

2. had heard
3. had decided
4. had won
5. had realized
6. had worked
7. had had
8. had developed
9. hadn't reached
10. had moved
11. had become
12. hadn't listened
13. had agreed
14. had been
15. had brought
16. had transformed

EXERCISE 3

2. Had he practiced; No, he hadn't.
3. Had he met; Yes, he had.
4. Had he called; No, he hadn't.
5. Had he done; No, he hadn't.
6. Had he started; Yes, he had.
7. Had he checked; Yes, he had.

EXERCISE 4

2. hadn't been doing
3. had been raining
4. had been eating
5. hadn't been drinking
6. had been crying
7. had been laughing
8. had been washing OR had been doing
9. had been listening
10. hadn't been paying

EXERCISE 5

2. How long had he been living in New York when he finally received a recording contract?
3. Had he really been working as a cook in a fast-food restaurant when he got his first job as a musician?
4. Where had he been studying when he decided to enroll at the Berklee School of Music?
5. Why had he been taking courses in accounting when he began his music classes?
6. How long had he been playing piano when he realized he wanted to be a professional musician?
7. Had he been looking for ways to help young musicians for a long time when he established his new scholarship program?

EXERCISE 6

2. had begun
3. had been studying
4. had received
5. had heard
6. had been pushing
7. had been
8. had been working
9. had been starring
10. had been recording
11. had had
12. had been waiting

EXERCISE 7

2. After she had lost the *Star Search* competition, she signed a contract with Columbia Records.
3. She had been working at Columbia Records for several years by the time she was in an ad for L'Oréal cosmetics.
4. Beyoncé made the comedy *Austin Powers in Goldmember* after she had filmed an MTV movie.
5. When she sang in a Pepsi ad, she had already done ads for L'Oréal.

6. By the time she celebrated her 25th birthday, she had already started a clothing company with her mother.
7. She had been acting for five years when she starred in *Dream Girls*.
8. She had become internationally famous before she got married to Jay-Z.
9. When she finished the movie *Obsessed*, she had already performed at a Barack Obama presidential celebration.
10. By the time she set a record by winning six Grammy awards in one night, she had already earned millions from recording, movie, and advertising contracts.

EXERCISE 8

My assignment for tonight was to see Lang Lang at Symphony Center. To be honest, I hadn't expected
much before I ~~had gone~~ *went* to the concert. In fact, I
hadn't been ~~look~~ *looking* forward to it at all. But then Lang Lang got my attention with his first two pieces.

By intermission, I had totally ~~change~~ *changed* my mind.
Lang Lang ~~had played just~~ *had just played* "Hungarian Rhapsody No. 2," and the audience had gone wild. I had
~~been hearing~~ *heard* Lizst's composition many times before,
but not like that. By the time he ~~finishes~~ *finished* playing, everyone in the audience had jumped to their feet and had started clapping enthusiastically. And the
best part of the concert ~~had~~ *hadn't* started yet.

After intermission, Lang Lang invited several young musicians to join him on the stage. All of
them had ~~been winning~~ *won* a scholarship from the Lang Lang International Music Foundation. When each
child performed, I ~~had felt~~ *felt* their excitement and their passion for music. It was wonderful to see that talented children could have a chance to succeed, regardless of their ethnic background or financial situation.

Superstar quality was certainly on display tonight. As I left Symphony Center, I had to ask myself a question. Lang Lang was absolutely
incredible. Why ~~I had~~ *had I* taken so long to find out about him?

EXERCISE 9

Answers will vary.

EXERCISE 1

2. I'll bring
3. Are you taking
4. He's going to miss; we won't be
5. We're attending; does the conference start
6. I'll answer
7. It's going to fall
8. We're going to see; he won't apply
9. Our plane leaves; It's going to break

EXERCISE 2

2. will be enjoying
3. won't be harming
4. aren't going to be using
5. are going to be taking advantage of
6. will be working
7. are going to be doing
8. won't be driving
9. are going to be traveling
10. will be walking
11. is going to be blowing
12. will be drinking
13. is going to be cleaning
14. will be burning
15. will be collecting
16. will be paying
17. are going to be trying

EXERCISE 3

2. Will the company (OR it) be paying for my wife's airfare? Yes, we will.
3. are you going to be traveling alone? No, I'm not.
4. are you going to be doing?
5. will you be stopping at the consulate office today? No, I won't.
6. Is she going to be sending the travel documents soon? Yes, she is.
7. will we be living in?
8. will we be getting to the airport?

EXERCISE 4

2. will be talking to . . . calls the electric company
3. will be buying everything . . . does research about vertical farms
4. tries to find Toni's birthday gift . . . will be eating lunch
5. will be attending a meeting for new employees . . . visits
6. meets . . . will be taking the dog to Brigitte's house
7. will be picking up a surprise cake . . . prepares dinner
8. finishes packing . . . will be putting winter clothes

EXERCISE 5

It's 11:00 P.M. now. ~~I go~~ *I'm going* to bed in a few minutes, but I'm afraid that I won't get much sleep tonight. I'll be tired when I ~~will~~ get up, but I can't stop thinking about my new job. Toni has our last day here completely planned. In the morning, we're going *to* have breakfast with friends and family. Then we're taking care of a few last-minute errands. Our plane ~~will leave~~ *leaves* at 5:00 P.M., and Toni has already made a reservation for a taxi at 2:00. I'm really excited. At this time tomorrow, Toni and I will be ~~sit~~ *sitting* on the airplane on our way to Abu Dhabi. If I know Toni, she ~~is~~ *will be* OR *is going to be* enjoying a movie while I ~~will~~ try to catch up on my sleep. Oh, no, I hear thunder. It ~~will~~ *'s going to* rain, so I'd better close all the windows. Maybe ~~I'm going to~~ *I'll* watch the rain for a while. It ~~'s~~ *'ll be* OR *'s going to be* a long time before I see rain again.

EXERCISE 6

Answers will vary.

EXERCISE 1

2. will have taken
3. will have helped
4. 'll have used
5. 'll have purchased
6. 'll have wrapped
7. won't have planned
8. won't have decided
9. 'll have argued
10. 'll have accomplished
11. won't have wasted
12. 'll have finished
13. 'll have had
14. 'll have participated
15. (will have) redecorated
16. 'll have made
17. 'll have explained

EXERCISE 2

3. A: How many rooms will Arnie have painted by August 5?
   B: He'll have painted three rooms.
4. A: When will Arnie have finished all the painting?
   B: He'll have finished the painting by August 14.
5. A: Will Aida have started driving the carpool by August 6?
   B: Yes, she will (have).
6. A: On August 16, will Arnie have left for his dentist appointment by 4:00?
   B: Yes, he will (have).
7. A: Will Aida have unpacked all the fall clothing by August 23?
   B: No, she won't (have).

8. A: How many quarts of blueberries will Corrie have picked by August 19?

   B: She'll have picked three quarts of blueberries.

9. A: How many pies will Aida have baked by August 21?

   B: She'll have baked six pies.

10. A: Will they have finished packing for the trip by August 31?

   B: Yes, they will (have).

EXERCISE 3

2. Arnie starts the family get-together menu, Corrie and Marsha will have been picking vegetables

3. Aida will have called Arnie's sister . . . Arnie does the menu

4. Arnie will have met with the family's banker . . . Aida pays the monthly credit card bills

5. Aida finishes the fall clothes, she will have been working on them

6. the Community Center bake sale takes place . . . Corrie and Marsha won't have finished . . .

7. Arnie will have been planning his special menu . . . he goes shopping

8. the family travels to Aunt Irene's house, they will have had a very productive month

EXERCISE 4

                    have

By your next birthday, will you ‸made your

                 wasted

dreams come true, or will you have ~~waste~~ another 12

                      enjoying

months of your life? Will others have been ~~enjoy~~ fame and fortune for years when you finally decide to take action? Don't wait any longer. The secret to your success is in our new book *Making Time for a*

                   will have

Happy Future. We guarantee that you ~~have~~ found the formula for a better life by the time you ~~will~~ finish the last page of our incredible book. Without a

              seen

doubt, you'll have ~~seeing~~ the big difference that time management can make. Even better, you'll have paid only $49.95 (plus tax and shipping and handling) when you receive the key to your future. Your friends

               yet.

will not have received ~~yet~~ this offer. But you must act fast. Make your purchase now, or ‸by this time next

      will

week, you ‸have missed the opportunity of a lifetime!

EXERCISE 5

Answers will vary.

EXERCISE 1

2. doesn't it?; No, it doesn't.
3. is it?; No, it isn't.
4. haven't you?; Yes, I have.
5. does it?; Yes, it does.
6. didn't you?; Yes, I did.
7. doesn't it?; Yes, it does.
8. can I?; Yes, you can.
9. will they?; No, they won't.
10. don't you?; Yes, I do.

EXERCISE 2

2. Didn't Greenwood build a public beach? No, it didn't.
3. Aren't there historic structures in Greenwood? Yes, there are.
4. Can't you see live theater performances in Greenwood? No, you can't.
5. Don't people in Greenwood shop at a nearby mall? Yes, they do.
6. Isn't the average rent in Greenwood under $800? Yes, it is.
7. Hasn't Greenwood been a town for more than a hundred years? Yes, it has.
8. Aren't they going to build a baseball stadium in Greenwood? Yes, they are.

EXERCISE 3

A. 3. isn't it

B. 1. have you
  2. Didn't . . . fill out
  3. shouldn't we

C. 1. Isn't
  2. Didn't . . . use to be
  3. had it

D. 1. aren't they
  2. have you
  3. Can't . . . take

EXERCISE 4

3. This is a good building, isn't it? OR Isn't this a good building?
4. The owner takes good care of it, doesn't he? OR Doesn't the owner take good care of it?
5. He's just finished renovations on the lobby, hasn't he? OR Hasn't he just finished renovations on the lobby?
6. He didn't paint our apartment before we moved in, did he?
7. He doesn't talk very much, does he?
8. The rent won't increase next year, will it?
9. Some new people will be moving into Apartment 1B, won't they? OR Won't some new people be moving into Apartment 1B?
10. This is a really nice place to live, isn't it? OR Isn't this a really nice place to live?

EXERCISE 5

Mariam: You own this building, ~~didn't~~ *don't* you?

Owner: Yes. And you've been living next door for about a year now, ~~have~~ *haven't* you?

Mariam: That's right. But I'm interested in moving. There's a vacant apartment in your building, isn't ~~it~~ *there*?

Owner: Yes. It's a one-bedroom on the fourth floor. The rent is $900 a month, plus utilities.

Mariam: Wow! That's a lot of money, isn't it? ~~Could you not~~ *Couldn't you* lower the rent a little?

Owner: Wait a minute! You came over here to talk to me, ~~haven't~~ *didn't* you? You want to live here, don't you?

Mariam: ~~No.~~ *Yes.* I love this building. It would be perfect for me, but I can't pay $900 a month.

Owner: But this is an historic structure. I was originally planning to charge $1,000 a month.

Mariam: I know. The history is what attracted me in the first place. But the elevator isn't working, ~~isn't~~ *is* it?

Owner: No, it isn't. OK, so if I lower the rent, you'll do some things in the apartment like painting, won't ~~they~~ *you*?

Mariam: Definitely. And I'm going to pay $700 a month, ~~amn't~~ *aren't* I?

Owner: OK, OK. And you can move in next weekend, ~~can~~ *can't* you?

Mariam: It's a deal!

EXERCISE 6

Answers will vary.

UNIT 8 (pages 44–48)

EXERCISE 1

2. isn't
3. hasn't
4. so
5. Neither
6. won't
7. and
8. either
9. did Olga
10. too

EXERCISE 2

A.
2. didn't either
3. am too
4. did too
5. so did
6. but . . . don't

B.
1. but . . . didn't
2. neither had
3. so did
4. but . . . wasn't

C.
1. are too
2. so will

EXERCISE 3

2. but Pleucadeuc wasn't
3. and neither does Beijing OR and Beijing doesn't either
4. but the Pleucadeuc and Beijing festivals are
5. and Pleucadeuc will too OR and so will Pleucadeuc
6. and so should participants at Pleucadeuc OR and participants at Pleucadeuc should too
7. and the Beijing festival doesn't either OR and neither does the Beijing festival
8. and so does Pleucadeuc OR and Pleucadeuc does too
9. but triplets, quads, and quints don't
10. and neither did Beijing OR and Beijing didn't either
11. and their families have too OR and so have their families

EXERCISE 4

Twinsburg really knows how to throw a party! I went to the festival in 2010. My twin sister and my cousins ~~do~~ *did* too. We had a great time. I really enjoyed the line dancing, and so did my sister. I had never done that kind of dancing before, but once I started, I couldn't stop, and neither ~~can~~ *could* she. To be honest, I was hoping to see a cute guy twin at the dance, and my sister ~~did~~ *was* too, but we were out of luck. I didn't meet anyone, and my sister didn't ~~neither~~ *either*. But we still had fun. Our favorite part was the picnic on Friday night. I loved seeing all the other twins there, *my sister did too* OR *so did my sister* and ~~did my sister too~~.

I have always liked being a twin, but my sister ~~has~~ *hasn't*. The Twinsburg festival changed all that. By Saturday morning, she was really excited. Of course I was too. We couldn't wait for the Double-Take Parade to start. My sister and I both marched in the parade. I felt really proud and excited to be a part of it. ~~So she did~~ *And so did she* OR *And she did too*.

Attending the Twins Day Festival with my sister may be a factor in why I liked it so much, but my cousins aren't twins, and they can't wait to go back. My sister and I think the festival is fantastic, and they ~~are~~ *do* too.

EXERCISE 5

UNIT 9 (pages 49–55)

EXERCISE 1

3. to watch
4. to watch
5. to watch
6. to watch OR watching
7. to watch
8. watching
9. to watch
10. watching
11. to watch OR watching
12. watching
13. watching
14. watching
15. to watch
16. watching
17. watching
18. watching
19. to watch
20. to watch

EXERCISE 2

2. watching
3. to recall
4. hearing
5. to calm
6. Sponsoring
7. to limit
8. to participate
9. creating
10. to preview
11. having
12. to believe
13. viewing
14. interacting
15. to behave
16. to produce
17. limiting OR to limit
18. not permitting
19. to watch
20. to understand
21. making
22. to develop
23. (to) get rid of
24. to offer
25. to advertise
26. to decrease
27. not to continue
28. to avoid OR avoiding
29. not to pay
30. to investigate
31. to schedule
32. turning on

EXERCISE 3

2. unwilling OR not willing to change
3. used to putting
4. fed up with seeing
5. likely to hit
6. force . . . to rate
7. hesitate to tell
8. decided to run
9. stopped showing
10. dislike turning off
11. insist on changing
12. forbid . . . to turn on
13. permit . . . to tune in
14. consider using
15. advise . . . to do
16. keep communicating
17. hesitate to ask
18. agreeing to speak

EXERCISE 4

2. A V-chip interferes with Annie's (OR Annie) watching violent shows.
3. The show encourages them to get interested in books.
4. Her father told Jennifer not to watch cop shows anymore.
5. The teacher recommended their watching news for children.
6. Bob didn't (OR doesn't) remember their (OR them) seeing that game.
7. Sharif's parents persuaded him not to watch the cartoon.
8. The mother insisted on Sara's (OR Sara) turning off the TV.
9. Aziza wanted (OR wants) Ben to change the channel.
10. Nick can't get used to Paul's (OR Paul) watching a Spanish-language news program.

EXERCISE 5

            hearing
I'm tired of ~~hear~~ that violence on TV causes violence at home, in school, and on the streets. Almost all young people watch TV, but not all of them are involved in committing crimes! In fact,
           to act
very few people choose ~~acting~~ in violent ways.
Watching
~~To watch~~ TV, therefore, is not the cause.
    Groups like the American Medical Society
               telling
should stop making a point of ~~to tell~~ people what
        to live
to watch. If we want ~~living~~ in a free society, it is
       to have
necessary ~~having~~ freedom of choice. Children need
to learn
~~learn~~ values from their parents. It should be the
             to decide
parents' responsibility alone ~~deciding~~ what their child can or cannot watch. The government and
              interfering
other interest groups should avoid ~~to interfere~~ in these personal decisions. Limiting our freedom of choice is not the answer. If parents teach their
       to respect   *watching*
children ~~respecting~~ life, children can enjoy ~~to watch~~ TV without any negative effects.

EXERCISE 6

EXERCISE 1

2. let	7. get	12. help
3. help	8. help	13. have
4. makes	9. gets	14. make
5. make	10. let	
6. get	11. makes	

EXERCISE 2

2. you keep	9. her play
3. you (to) decide	10. him (to) adjust
4. them give	11. him spend
5. her to do	12. him to obey
6. them take care of	13. him understand
7. them to realize	14. you (to) relax
8. him to calm down	15. us provide

EXERCISE 3

2. got him to agree to adopt a dog or a cat.
3. let him make the choice.
4. made him do some research on pet care.
5. didn't help him do the research. OR didn't help him to do the research.
6. got her to fill out and sign the adoption application forms.
7. had him explain the adoption process (to her).
8. didn't make him pay the adoption fees.

EXERCISE 4

Thanks for staying in touch. Your emails always make me ~~to~~ *smile* even when I'm feeling stressed. Knowing that I have a good friend like you really helps me ~~relaxing~~ *relax* and not take things so seriously.

At the end of last semester, my roommates and I decided to get a dog. Actually, my roommates made the decision and then got me *to* go along with it. I made them promise to take care of the dog, but guess who's doing most of the work?! Don't misunderstand me. I love Ellie and appreciate what a great companion she is. I take her for a walk every morning and every night and ~~make~~ *let* her run and play in the park near our apartment as often as I can because I know how much she enjoys it. Still, I wish I could have my roommates ~~to~~ *spend* just an hour a week with "our" dog. At this point, I can't even get them ~~feeding~~ *to feed* Ellie, and now they want to move to an

apartment complex that won't let us ~~to have~~ *have* a dog. I think I'm going to have to choose whether to live with my roommates or with Ellie—and I think I'm going to choose Ellie!

EXERCISE 5

Answers will vary.

EXERCISE 1

2. up	7. over	12. down
3. over	8. out	13. up
4. ahead	9. back	14. down
5. out	10. out	15. off
6. down	11. up	16. up

EXERCISE 2

2. cut down	7. gets together
3. put together	8. give out
4. burns up	9. go out
5. sets up	10. go back
6. puts on	11. throws away

EXERCISE 3

A. 2. pick them out
B. 1. empty out the money and everything else in your pockets
   2. throw it away
C. 1. set the firecrackers off
   2. keeps them away
D. 1. hanging these streamers up
   2. set it up
E. 1. write down all of the resolutions that I make each year
   2. gave them up

EXERCISE 4

Wake ~~out~~ *up* earlier. (No later than 7:30!)
Work out at the gym at least 3 times a week.

Lose 5 pounds. (Give ~~over~~ *up* eating so many desserts.)

Be more conscious of the environment:
—Don't throw ~~down~~ *away* OR *out* newspapers. Recycle them.
—Save energy. Turn ~~on~~ *off* OR *out* the lights and TV when I leave the apartment.

Straighten up my room and make it more comfortable:

—Hang ~~out~~ *up* my clothes when I take ~~off them~~ *them off*.

—Put my books back where they belong.

—Give ^*away* some of my old books and clothing that I no longer wear ~~away~~.

—Read about feng shui theory to increase positive energy.

Don't put off doing my math homework even when the problems seem complex. Finish the assignments, and hand ~~in them~~ *them in* on time!

Read more.

Use the dictionary more. (Look ~~over~~ *up* words I don't know.)

When someone calls and leaves a message, call them back right away. Don't put ~~off it~~ *it off*!

Get to know my neighbors. Ask them ^*over* for coffee ~~over~~.

EXERCISE 5

Answers will vary.

UNIT 12 (pages 66–71)

EXERCISE 1

2. over	10. down
3. out	11. into
4. off	12. back
5. in (on) OR by	13. out
6. out	14. on
7. on OR up	15. out
8. into	16. down
9. up	

EXERCISE 2

A. 2. figured out
  3. catch on
  4. turning on
  5. teamed up with
  6. help . . . out
  7. go off
  8. takes away
  9. turn . . . off

B. 1. keep up with
  2. end up
  3. put . . . away
  4. use up
  5. found out
  6. pick out
  7. look over
  8. watch out for

EXERCISE 3

2. get along (well) with him
3. run into her
4. straighten it up
5. gotten together with them
6. pick them out OR pick some out
7. count on them
8. bring it out
9. picked it up
10. turn it down
11. cover them up
12. stuck to it
13. put them away
14. turn it on
15. figure it out

EXERCISE 4

EXERCISE 5

In my opinion, drivers should hang ~~on~~ *up* their phones and turn off ^*them* ~~them~~ the minute they get in their cars. This is the best way to eliminate some of the careless accidents on the streets of our city. After all, is it more important to keep up ^*with* your friends and business associates ~~with~~ or save lives and money? I have looked into this matter and found ^*out* some alarming statistics on mobile phones and accidents ~~out~~. Research from the National Safety Council points out that cell phones and texting cause 1.6 million accidents each year. Clearly, it's time for drivers to get ~~in~~ *off* the phone. And it's time for lawmakers to come ~~over~~ up with a plan to make all phone use by motorists illegal, including the use of headsets and other hands-free technology. They must create a law to turn into ~~our streets~~ our streets safe places for drivers and pedestrians alike. Then the local authorities must carry out it ~~it~~.

EXERCISE 6

Answers will vary.

UNIT 13 (pages 72–77)

EXERCISE 1

2. Some people assume we are born with personality traits which control all our feelings and actions.
3. Researchers whose work is in the field of positive psychology contradict that idea.
4. Positive psychologists offer practical advice for anyone who wants a better chance of being happy.
5. One activity that helps to improve feelings of happiness is making a list of three good things in your life.
6. Having a close friend who cares about you also increases the possibility of happiness.
7. Interestingly, a mother whose children are grown doesn't seem to be any happier than a woman with no children.

EXERCISE 2

2. whose	8. that	14. whose
3. that	9. that	15. that
4. who	10. which	16. whose
5. which	11. who	17. which
6. that	12. that	18. that
7. which	13. who	

EXERCISE 3

2. laugh	12. that has
3. plan	13. that OR which bring
4. that keeps	14. which increases
5. whose . . . continue	15. decreases
6. who is	16. that OR which makes
7. which . . . makes	17. that helps
8. who respects	18. that OR which lasts
9. who doesn't mind	19. who do
10. that OR who feel	20. which feels
11. who OR that find	

EXERCISE 4

2. She was visiting her favorite aunt, whose apartment was right across from mine.
3. I was immediately attracted to Rebecca because of her unique smile, which was full of warmth and good humor.
4. I could see that Rebecca, whose interests were similar to mine, had a fun-loving personality.
5. Ballroom dancing, which was very popular in those days, was one of our favorite activities.
6. We also enjoyed playing cards with some of our close friends who (OR that) lived in the neighborhood.
7. Our friend Mike, who was a professional skier, taught us how to ski.
8. We got married in a ski lodge that (OR which) was in Vermont.
9. Our marriage, which means a lot to us both, has grown through the years.
10. The love and companionship that (OR which) make us very happy have gotten stronger.
11. Even the bad things that (OR which) have happened have brought us closer together.
12. I really love Rebecca, who makes me feel truly happy.

EXERCISE 5

Psychological research that ~~focus~~ focuses on happiness requires a tool that can measure a person's feelings. A number of well-known researchers who ~~they~~ collect this type of data claim to have a simple method that ~~work~~ works well. They ask just one question, which is "How happy are you?" People ~~which~~ who OR that respond to the question usually give their answer with a number. For example, on a scale of 1–10, a 1 would be "extremely unhappy" and a 10 would be "extremely happy." Professor Ed Diener, ~~that~~ who is a leading U.S. psychologist, says the method is surprisingly effective because it produces answers that ~~is~~ are honest and real. Of course there may be someone ~~who~~ whose feelings change throughout the day, so there is a related type of measurement ~~who~~ that OR which uses handheld computers to send messages to research participants to find out what they are doing at different times and what their mood is. Technology is also important for scientists ~~which~~ who OR that make a connection between happiness and the human body. When they see a person whose skin temperature ~~have~~ has risen, they know the person is happy. This group of researchers believes their method of measuring happiness through body heat, blood pressure, heart rate, and brain waves is quite effective.

EXERCISE 6

Answers will vary.

UNIT 14 (pages 78–83)

EXERCISE 1

2. that	10. that	18. whom
3. which	11. who	19. that
4. which	12. whom	20. whose
5. that	13. whose	21. where
6. which	14. where	22. whose
7. when	15. whose	23. when
8. that	16. that	24. whom
9. which	17. whose	

EXERCISE 2

2. where	15. supported
3. thanks	16. which
4. whose	17. praised
5. finds, has found, OR found	18. which
	19. inserted
6. which OR that	20. whom
7. writes	21. feels
8. which OR that	22. whom
9. read	23. dedicates OR has dedicated
10. which OR that	
11. face	24. where
12. when	25. has
13. runs out of OR has run out of	26. which OR that
	27. are supposed to
14. when	

EXERCISE 3

2. *The Clan of the Cave Bear*, which Auel started researching in 1977, tells the story of a clan of prehistoric people.

3. It took a lot of work to learn about these prehistoric people, whose lives Auel wanted to understand.

4. The clan lived during the Ice Age, when glaciers covered large parts of the Earth.

5. The people lived near the shores of the Black Sea, where there are a lot of large caves.

6. The clan made their home in a large cave where bears had lived.

7. The task of hunting, which the men were responsible for, had great importance in the life of the Cave Bear Clan. OR The task of hunting, for which the men were responsible, had great importance in the life of the Cave Bear Clan.

8. One aspect of their lives which (OR that) Auel describes well was their technical skill.

9. She learned some of the arts that (OR which) prehistoric people had practiced.

10. In her preface, Auel thanks a man with whom she studied the art of making stone tools. OR Auel thanks a man who (OR whom) (OR that) she studied the art of making stone tools with.

11. She also thanks an Arctic survival expert who (OR whom) (OR that) she met while she was doing research.

12. He taught her to make a snow cave on Mt. Hood, where she spent one January night.

13. She went through a difficult time when she couldn't write.

14. A fiction writer whose lecture she attended inspired her to finish her book.

15. Jean Auel's novel, which she published in 1980, remains popular in translations around the world.

EXERCISE 4

Sentence 8: One aspect of their lives Auel describes well was their technical skill.

Sentence 9: She learned some of the arts prehistoric people had practiced.

Sentence 10: In her preface, Auel thanks a man she studied the art of making stone tools with.

Sentence 11: She also thanks an Arctic survival expert she met while she was doing research.

EXERCISE 5

For my book report, I read *The Clan of the Cave Bear*, ~~that~~ *which* Jean M. Auel wrote after several years of research. In this novel about the life of prehistoric people, the main character is Ayla. She is found by a wandering clan after an earthquake kills her family. The same earthquake destroyed the cave in which this clan had lived, and they are searching for another home. The clan leader wants to leave Ayla to die. She is an Other—a human ~~which~~ *whose* language and culture his clan doesn't understand. However, the leader's sister Iza ^ Ayla soon calls Mother, adopts her. *who* OR *whom*

The story takes place at a time ~~where~~ *when* human beings are still evolving. Ayla is a new kind of human. Her brain, which she can use ~~it~~ to predict and make plans, is different from Iza's and other clan members'. Their brains are adapted to memory, not new learning, ~~whom~~ *which* they fear and distrust. At first, Ayla brings luck to the clan. She accidentally wanders into a place where they find a large cave, perfect for their new home. She is educated by Iza, ~~who's~~ *whose* great knowledge everyone respects. The skills that Iza passes on to Ayla include healing and magic, as well as finding food, cooking, and sewing. However, Ayla's powers make it impossible for her to stay with the clan. She learns to hunt, a skill ~~where~~ *which* OR *that* OR *(pronoun deleted)* women are forbidden to practice. Her uncle, ~~that~~ *who* OR *whom* she loves very much, allows her to stay with the clan, but after he dies, she loses his protection. Another earthquake, for which she is blamed, destroys the clan's home, and she is forced to leave.

EXERCISE 6

Answers will vary.

UNIT 15 (pages 84–87)

EXERCISE 1

2. ability
3. necessity
4. assumption
5. necessity
6. ability
7. advice
8. advice
9. future possibility
10. assumption
11. necessity
12. prohibition
13. advice
14. prohibition
15. future possibility

EXERCISE 2

2. couldn't live
3. can protect
4. must know
5. may not remember
6. doesn't have to be
7. should choose
8. 're able to recall OR 'll be able to recall
9. might find out
10. ought to think
11. 'd better follow
12. could have
13. 've got to do
14. musn't give

EXERCISE 3

1. 'd better
2. Should; might; can't
3. have to; can
4. may not
5. must not; couldn't
6. must; ought to; can
7. 'd better not; wasn't able to
8. ought to; couldn't
9. can you; might
10. couldn't; must
11. can't; 've got to
12. could; must

EXERCISE 4

I must ~~to say~~ *say* that Karun is absolutely correct about good passwords. You ~~could~~ *might* not think they're important, but I'm here to tell you that you had better ~~not~~ pay attention to your online security. I had a major problem last year. I ~~didn't~~ *wasn't* able to use my credit card when I went shopping one day because someone had charged five or six big-screen TVs and airline tickets to my account and I had no more available credit. I couldn't believe it was happening to me. I ~~must~~ *had to* spend almost two months taking care of the problem, but I finally did. And I learned that this problem can ~~happened~~ *happen* to anyone, so we ~~don't~~ have to protect ourselves. I no longer have a "12345" password and you shouldn't use one either. ~~May~~ *Can* you think of a better way to protect your privacy—and your money?

EXERCISE 5

Answers will vary.

UNIT 16 (pages 88–92)

EXERCISE 1

2. could . . . have done
3. Should . . . have let
4. Yes, you should have
5. could have given
6. might have discussed
7. should . . . have handled
8. shouldn't have adjusted
9. ought to have faced
10. should have tried
11. Should . . . have ignored
12. No, you shouldn't have
13. ought to have told
14. might have acted
15. Should . . . have complained
16. No, you shouldn't have
17. ought to have been able to
18. shouldn't have spent
19. shouldn't have called
20. might have focused
21. could have admitted

EXERCISE 2

2. They ought to have created a budget with some "personal money" for each partner.
3. He might have treated her attitude with respect.
4. She shouldn't have accused him of being irresponsible OR irresponsibility.
5. They should have planned ahead.
6. They could have scheduled time alone with each other.
7. He shouldn't have sulked.
8. They might have started with small tasks.
9. They could have provided containers to help organize the toys.
10. He shouldn't have given up and done it himself.

EXERCISE 3

I think my new roommate and I have both
                    shouldn't
realized our mistakes. Reggie ~~should~~ have demanded
the biggest room in the apartment as soon as he
     to
arrived. He ought ^ have spoken to me first—after all,
I've lived here longer than he has. On the other hand,
    have shouted
I really shouldn't ~~shout~~ at him as soon as he asked
    controlled
me. I could have ~~control~~ my temper and just talked
to him about the problem first. I felt really bad about
that—until he invited friends over the night before
I had to take a test! Then I got so angry I couldn't
        asked   *ought to*
sleep. He might have ~~asks~~ me first! I ~~oughta~~ have
said something right away, but I didn't want to yell
again. Of course, some of my habits make Reggie
mad too. For example, I could've started washing my
dishes when he moved in, but I just let them pile up
in the sink. That was pretty gross—I definitely
       done   *should he have*
shouldn't have ~~did~~ that. But ~~should have he~~ dumped
                    have
all the dirty dishes in my bedroom? He might ^ found
a better way to tell me he was annoyed. Last week,
he wanted to talk about our problems. As soon
as we started, I realized we should have tried this
technique sooner. Things have worked out a lot
better since our discussion.

EXERCISE 4

Answers will vary.

EXERCISE 1

2. couldn't have
3. must have
4. may have
5. must have
6. must have
7. could have
8. may have
9. could have
10. couldn't have
11. had to have

EXERCISE 2

2. must not have been
3. had to have felt
4. must have occupied
5. may have traded
6. couldn't have lived
7. may not have lived
8. must have fought
9. may have been
10. might not have produced
11. could have gone
12. might not have had
13. may have suffered
14. could have led
15. might have destroyed
16. could have been

EXERCISE 3

2. It must have been
3. He might have
4. He may have
5. She could have
6. It must have been
7. They must have
8. He might not have been
9. It couldn't have been

EXERCISE 4

2. might have finished her degree
3. couldn't have climbed that pyramid
4. may have taken everything to the local museum
5. must not have understood the importance of their discoveries
6. might not have gotten so interested in the Maya
7. couldn't have been more people
8. had to have developed a system of numbers
9. could have painted a picture of a warrior

EXERCISE 5

I sent you an email last week, but I never heard
                      received
back from you. You might not have ~~receive~~ it, or you
     have
may ~~had~~ been too busy to respond. I understand. It's
not easy to keep in touch when you're traveling.

Your father and I got your postcard of the Mayan temple. You had to have enjoyed that part of your trip. I know how interested you are in archeology. I saw a program on television a while ago about the Maya. Actually, it was about the Red Queen. The scientists who found her must ~~not~~ have been really surprised because it was the first time anyone had discovered the body of a Mayan woman in a royal tomb. They're still trying to figure out who she was.

Because she was buried in a way similar to Mayan kings, she must *have* ~~has~~ belonged to the royal family, but that doesn't completely solve the mystery of her identity. The red dust that covered her body made the investigation difficult. At first, scientists thought she could have been one of three women. I found their names on a Red Queen website—Yohl Ik Nal, Zak Kuk, and Tzakbu Ajaw.

After careful research, the scientists decided the woman had lived sometime during the 7th century, which meant it was impossible for her to be Yohl Ik Nal. It *couldn't have* ~~might not have~~ been her because Yohl Ik Nal died earlier than that. They also eliminated Zak Kuk, the mother of Pacal II, because the DNA in the body of the Red Queen was different from the DNA in the body of King Pacal II. There was no biological connection between them, so Zak Kuk could *n't* have been the Red Queen either. The last woman, Tzakbu Ajaw, *might have* OR *may have* OR *could have* ~~must have~~ been the Red Queen, but the researchers don't have enough information to be sure. Tzakbu Ajaw was the mother of Pacal II's children, but their bodies have not been found yet, so there is no DNA to compare.

You might have *found* ~~find~~ out something more about the Red Queen when you visited the Mayan temples. If you did, let me know. But no matter what, please call me, text me, or email me. I miss you!

EXERCISE 6

Answers will vary.

UNIT 18 (pages 101–106)

EXERCISE 1

3. Several employees were fired as a result of the mistake.
4. An article about the Philippines was published a decade ago.

5. Al Baker wrote the article.
6. They frequently hire new editors at the magazine.
7. Marla Jacobson was interviewed by two of the new editors.
8. They gave Marla an assignment on the Philippines.
9. The article was researched thoroughly by Marla.
10. The new article fascinated our readers.

EXERCISE 2

2. were called	7. were created
3. is not known	8. are populated
4. is made up	9. are not inhabited
5. are considered	10. are represented
6. were formed	

EXERCISE 3

3. are inhabited	8. cover
4. are found	9. contain
5. damage	10. are found
6. cause	11. are used
7. was covered	12. exist

EXERCISE 4

3. were followed by groups from Indonesia
4. are spoken
5. are understood by speakers of other dialects
6. was declared by President Manuel Quezon
7. is spoken by more than 70 million people
8. is taught
9. are spoken (by people)
10. is used

EXERCISE 5

3. Where are fruits and nuts grown? They're grown in the north (OR northeast) and in the central part of the country.
4. Where is logging done? It's done in the east (OR southeast).
5. What animals are raised? Sheep, cattle, and llamas are raised.
6. Are llamas found in the east? No, they aren't.
7. Are potatoes grown? Yes, they are.
8. Where is rubber produced? It's produced in the north.
9. Where is oil found? It's found in the south, east, and west (OR northwest).
10. Is wheat grown in the north? No, it isn't.
11. Are cattle raised in the east? Yes, they are.

EXERCISE 6

Our mission is to bring you the world's great

architecture, and in this issue, our spotlight is ~~focus~~ *focused*

on India. The Taj Mahal, which is ~~locates~~ *located* in northern

India, is considered one of the eight wonders of

the world. It was built ~~by builders~~ for the Mughal

emperor Shah Jahan. The emperor ~~was~~ felt great

sadness when his wife Mumtaz Mahal died during

the birth of their fourteenth child in 1631, and the

Taj Mahal ~~were~~ *was* created as a symbol of his eternal

love. The incredible structure, which was ~~finish~~ *finished* in

approximately 1653, contains examples of Persian,

Islamic, and Indian architecture, and in 1983, it ~~was~~

became a UNESCO World Heritage Site.

The romance and beauty of Indian architecture

don't stop with the Taj Mahal. Magnificent

buildings *are* found throughout India, and you'll see

marvelous examples in the photos and articles in this

issue of our magazine. I'm sure that, like me, you'll

enjoy them all.

EXERCISE 7

Answers will vary.

UNIT 19 (pages 107–111)

EXERCISE 1

2. Some new airports may be constructed on islands.
3. They might put passenger facilities on decks under the runways.
4. A lot of space could be saved that way.
5. The Japanese had to build an island airport in Osaka Bay.
6. At the old airport, all the air traffic couldn't be handled.
7. Huge amounts of earth had to be moved from nearby mountains.
8. International visitors will be impressed by Hong Kong's island airport.
9. Travelers can reach the airport easily.
10. Before, Lantau could be reached only by ferry.

EXERCISE 2

2. can be connected
3. may be started
4. can be carried
5. may not be driven
6. are able to be transported
7. couldn't be done
8. might be built
9. must be crossed
10. have to be developed
11. are going to be linked
12. might be added
13. could be joined
14. will be called
15. might not be fulfilled
16. can't be avoided
17. will be solved

EXERCISE 3

2. No, they don't
3. Should . . . be obtained
4. Yes, they should
5. can . . . be made
6. Yes, they can
7. will . . . be mailed
8. No, they won't
9. Is. . . going to be offered
10. Yes, it is
11. Can . . . be purchased
12. Yes, it can

EXERCISE 4

If you like to reach for the stars when it comes

to travel, you may *be* interested in a trip to space. Of

course, your choices for space travel will be ~~limit~~ *limited*

by the amount of money you can spend, but there's

something for everyone.

Space tourism became a reality in 2001 for

travelers with big bank accounts. The more than $20

million cost of a trip to the International Space

Station could *be* paid only by millionaires like U.S.

businessman Dennis Tito or Canadian Guy Laliberté,

the founder of Cirque du Soleil. Now comes the news

that tourists will be ~~taking~~ *taken* into suborbital space by

Virgin Galactic. The six travelers and two pilots on

the Virgin Galactic flights can't remain in space for

an extended period of time, and their spaceship

won't orbit the Earth. However, they will be ~~shoot~~ *shot*

by a rocket to a height of 68 miles, where there will

be a true outer space experience. At that height, the

blackness of space can be seen and in it the curved

                                                be
shape of the planet Earth. Spacesuits must ~~been~~
worn at all times, but seat belts can be removed for
about four or five minutes to allow travelers to enjoy
the feeling of floating in zero gravity. According to
reports, 335 tickets at a cost of $200,000 each have
already been reserved.

    If $200,000 is still beyond your budget, your
                                          don't
dreams of an out-of-this-world experience ^have
to be forgotten. A half-day "Astronaut Training
Experience" is available at NASA's Kennedy Space
Center near Orlando, Florida, for $145. Even better,
                     be
your name can ^put on a microchip that is part of a
future NASA research project for free. Go to NASA's
website for more information.

EXERCISE 5

Answers will vary.

UNIT 20 (pages 112–117)

EXERCISE 1

2. I'm having (OR getting) my computer repaired.
3. I had (OR got) my car checked by my favorite mechanic at Majestic Motors.
4. We've just had (OR gotten) our windows cleaned.
5. We're going to have (OR get) our grass cut.
6. We must have (OR get) our house painted.
7. We should have (OR get) our electrical wiring checked.
8. We will probably have (OR get) most of the work on our house done by Northtown Contractors.
9. We might have (OR get) a new porch built (by them) too.
10. The neighbors had better have (OR get) the dead tree removed from their yard.

EXERCISE 2

2. have . . . completed
3. have . . . done
4. get . . . tested
5. have . . . replaced
6. have . . . investigated
7. had . . . installed
8. get . . . replaced
9. didn't have . . . done
10. had . . . tested
11. have . . . checked out
12. have . . . stopped
13. have . . . put
14. getting . . . publicized

EXERCISE 3

2. How often do you get it done?
3. Did you get it winterized?
4. Have you ever gotten snow tires put on?
5. Are you going to get (OR Will you get OR Are you getting) snow tires put on for the trip?
6. How many times have you gotten it checked since then?
7. Why do you get the work done there?

EXERCISE 4

3. He didn't have (OR get) the undercarriage inspected.
4. He had (OR got) the body and chassis lubricated.
5. He had (OR got) the air filter inspected.
6. He didn't have (OR get) the air filter replaced.
7. He didn't have (OR get) the tires rotated.
8. He didn't have (OR get) the timing and engine speed adjusted.
9. He had (OR got) the automatic transmission serviced.
10. He had (OR got) the cooling system flushed.

EXERCISE 5

              had
We've just ~~have~~ our furniture brought over from
the apartment, and we're really excited about
moving into our "new" (but very old) house. A
                                            built
19th-century millionaire had this place ~~build~~ for
his daughter ~~by a builder~~. We were able to afford
                                            have
it because it's a real "fixer-upper." It needs to ~~has~~
a lot of work done. We've already gotten the roof
fixed   *painted*
~~fix~~, but we're not having the outside ~~painting~~ until
fall. The plumbers are doing some work now. It's a
complicated procedure, but they should finish soon.
                     the plumbing repaired
After we get ~~repaired the plumbing~~, we'll paint the
inside ourselves (we can't paint over those big water
stains until the plumbers leave). It sounds awful, but
just wait until you see it. There's a fireplace in every
                    getting
bedroom—we're ~~get~~ the chimneys cleaned before
winter. And the windows are huge. In fact, they're so
large that we can't wash them ourselves, so yesterday
              them done
we had ~~done them~~ professionally.

    As you can imagine, we've both been pretty busy,
but we'd love to see you. Are you brave enough to
visit us?

EXERCISE 6

Answers will vary.

EXERCISE 1

3. That's right.
4. That's wrong. If you travel in September, your ticket costs more than if you travel in October.
5. That's wrong. If you fly in May, you pay off-season rates.
6. That's wrong. If you buy a one-way ticket, you pay more than half the cost of a round-trip ticket.
7. That's right.
8. That's right.
9. That's wrong. If you leave from Washington, you pay the same fare as from Philadelphia.
10. That's wrong. If you fly from Philadelphia, you pay a lower fare than from Chicago.

EXERCISE 2

3. If you don't want to spend a lot of money getting around in Rome, take public transportation.
4. If you want to be smart consumers when you book this trip, get a package deal with both airfare and hotel included.
5. If you prefer small hotels, stay at a *pensione*.
6. If your husband is very interested in architecture, you must visit the Palazzo Ducale in Venice.
7. If you love opera, you should attend an open-air performance in Verona's Roman Arena.
8. If you're interested in seeing ancient ruins, you might want to consider a side trip to Ostia Antica.
9. If you plan to take a hair dryer and an electric shaver with you, don't forget to take a transformer and an adapter.
10. If you want to have a really good dinner your first night there, you should try Sabatini's.

EXERCISE 3

3. You should bring along copies of your prescriptions and keep them in a secure place if you take prescription medication.
4. Notify the flight attendant or train conductor if you feel sick on board a plane or train.
5. Call your own doctor if you are traveling in your own country when you feel sick.
6. Your hotel can recommend a doctor if you need medical attention in a foreign country.
7. If you experience chest pains, weakness in an arm or leg, or shortness of breath, get yourself to an emergency room.

8. If you're not sure how serious your symptoms are, assume they are serious and take appropriate steps.
9. Don't drive to the hospital if you need to go to the emergency room.
10. If you wear glasses, take an extra pair with you.

EXERCISE 4

- You ~~had~~ *have* a better chance of getting a good seat on the plane if you buy your ticket early.
- If you ~~took~~ *take* a nonstop flight, it is sometimes cheaper than a trip with plane changes. It's *when* you travel that really counts.
  ~~Your schedule is flexible, if you~~ *If your schedule is flexible, you* should take advantage of travel at off-peak hours.
- Be aware of airline policy about cancellations or changes in reservations. When you make a change in your travel plans, there are almost always extra fees.
- If you do online check-in from your home or hotel, the amount of time you stand in line at the airport decreases. Besides, you know that your seat on the plane is confirmed ~~,~~ if you have a boarding pass before arriving at the airport.
- You save both time and money when you travel light. You don't have to wait in line to check a bag before departure or pick it up at baggage claim if you ~~has~~ *have* just a carry-on bag and one personal item. Even better, if you bring no luggage to check, then there are no baggage fees to pay.
- Airline employees try to be helpful *if* OR *when* they see problems. However, there is sometimes nothing they can do. If you ~~needed~~ *need* to dispute anything, be as polite as possible. It's the best way to get great service.
- If you travel often, then you know what I mean with this next piece of advice. Wear shoes that you can take off and put on easily. Frequent fliers use this strategy to make things easier at the security checkpoint.
- If you're traveling internationally, you must have your passport and visa documents with you. Even if they are traveling in their own country, many experienced travelers ~~are carrying~~ *carry* their passport. It's the safest form of personal identification.

EXERCISE 5

Answers will vary.

EXERCISE 1

b. skip	g. will be	l. unless
c. unless	h. take	m. If
d. exercise	i. won't catch	n. go
e. If	j. has	
f. change	k. going to have	

EXERCISE 2

2. decide
3. will . . . know OR am . . . going to know
4. go
5. 'll . . . have OR 're . . . going to have
6. Will . . . be able to OR Am . . . going to be able to
7. look
8. Yes, you will. OR Yes, you are.
9. have
10. won't be OR aren't going to be OR 're not going to be
11. ends
12. 'll . . . find OR 're . . . going to find
13. see
14. will . . . tell OR is . . . going to tell
15. Yes, it will. OR Yes, it is.
16. set
17. 'll receive OR 're going to receive
18. shows up
19. will . . . be OR is . . . going to be
20. No, it won't. OR No, it isn't.
21. wash
22. 'll get OR 're going to get
23. want
24. won't do OR 're not going to do OR aren't going to do

EXERCISE 3

3. You'll have (OR You're going to have) trouble losing weight unless you get regular exercise.
4. You'll receive (OR You're going to receive) some health benefits if you eat carrots.
5. If you stop eating meat, you'll need (OR you're going to need) something to replace it in your diet.
6. If you have a cold, vitamin C will help (OR is going to help) relieve the symptoms.
7. You'll suffer (OR You're going to suffer) possible negative effects if your body gets too much vitamin A.
8. You won't get (OR You aren't going to get OR You're not going to get) sick if you don't drink exactly eight glasses of water a day.

9. You won't have (OR You aren't going to have OR You're not going to have) a problem going out with wet hair unless you're worried about feeling cold OR looking less than perfect.

EXERCISE 4

If you ~~will~~ want to be healthy, then you should stay positive. At least that's what new medical findings seem to say. According to researchers, if you handle stress well and have an attitude toward life that is positive overall, you _will_ ~~won't~~ live a longer, healthier life. In a recent study, adults were asked questions about stressful situations that they were unable to anticipate. For example, they might have been asked, "How _will you_ ~~you will~~ react if you are stuck in traffic?" or "What will you do if your boss _asks_ ~~will ask~~ you to start a big project right at the end of the day?" Researchers found that the people with enthusiastic and positive responses had fewer heart attacks over the next 10 years. In a similar study, scientists discovered that having a positive attitude toward the future made people 12 percent less likely to suffer a heart attack. Other research has also shown a connection between a positive attitude and good health. According to the studies, if people ~~will~~ approach life in a positive way, they'll be less likely to get a cold or the flu and more likely to have lower blood pressure.

Will a woman live longer if she develops a more positive attitude? Doctors won't really know _unless_ ~~if~~ more research is done, but many believe it's possible that a change in attitude will help. Doctors are confident of one thing. You'll feel mentally stronger _if_ you do things that you enjoy. So, if you like spending time with friends or playing sports, you should do it. And while you're at it, take care of yourself. If you get enough sleep, exercise, and eat right, you'll feel the connection between better health and a more positive attitude.

EXERCISE 5

Answers will vary.

EXERCISE 1

2. could sleep
3. were
4. offered
5. wouldn't eat
6. 'd be
7. had
8. 'd give
9. didn't need
10. 'd offer
11. weren't
12. didn't need
13. 'd share
14. could offer
15. had
16. would taste
17. would taste
18. put
19. had
20. added
21. would be
22. stirred
23. would be
24. knew
25. ate
26. 'd require

EXERCISE 2

2. We wish the soldiers wouldn't keep asking for our food.
3. We wish we didn't have to hide our food from them.
4. We wish we didn't need all our grain to feed the cows.
5. We wish all our beds weren't full.
6. We wish there were enough room for the soldiers.
7. We wish the king would come here to eat with us.
8. We wish we had a larger soup pot.
9. We wish we could have stone soup every day.

EXERCISE 3

2. If I had potatoes, I'd make potato soup.
3. If my apartment weren't small, I'd invite people over.
4. If steak weren't expensive, we'd eat it.
5. If my daughter weren't sick, I'd go shopping later today.
6. If I didn't have bad eyesight, I could join the army.
7. If the soup had seasoning in it, it wouldn't taste so bland.
8. If I knew the answer, I wouldn't be embarrassed now.
9. If I were rich, I'd take vacations.
10. If I had the recipe, I'd make stone soup.

EXERCISE 4

2. If I were you, I'd read a fairy tale.
3. If I were you, I'd try cabbage soup.
4. If I were you, I wouldn't add salt.
5. If I were you, I wouldn't ask for a raise.
6. If I were you, I wouldn't take her to see *Rambo VII* (OR to that movie).
7. If I were you, I'd move.
8. If I were you, I'd eat out.

EXERCISE 5

2. Who would look for us if we got lost?
3. Where would we go if it started to rain?
4. Would you be afraid if we saw a bear?
5. If you heard a loud growl, would you be scared?
6. What would you do if you were in my place?
7. What would we do if we ran out of food?
8. If we didn't have any more food, would we make stone soup?

EXERCISE 6

It's 11:00 P.M. and I'm still awake. I wish I ~~was~~ *were* home. If I ~~would be~~ *were* home, I would be asleep by now! But here I am in the middle of nowhere. I'm furious at myself for agreeing to go camping. My sleeping bag is really uncomfortable. If I were more comfortable, I ~~will~~ *would* be able to sleep. What ~~do~~ *would* my family think if they could see me now?

I'm cold, tired, and hungry. I wish I ~~have~~ *had* something to eat. But all the food is locked up in the van, and everyone else is sound asleep. If I ~~would have~~ *had* a book, I would read, but I didn't bring any books. Tonight, as we sat around the campfire, someone read a story called "Stone Soup." I'm so hungry that even stone soup sounds good to me. If I ~~know~~ *knew* the recipe, I ~~made~~ *would make* it.

Well, I'm getting tired of holding this flashlight (I wish I ~~would have~~ *had* a regular lamp!), so I think I'll try to fall asleep.

EXERCISE 7

Answers will vary.

EXERCISE 1

2. had stayed; might not have created
3. could have ended up; had agreed
4. had spoken; might have enjoyed
5. wouldn't have become; hadn't had
6. had used; wouldn't have been; might not have loved
7. would've made; hadn't started
8. 'd found

EXERCISE 2

2. had been
3. had found
4. might have been
5. hadn't earned
6. might . . . have seen
7. (might never have) owned
8. hadn't paid
9. would have had
10. hadn't given
11. wouldn't have survived
12. had gotten
13. could have paid
14. hadn't met
15. might have been
16. would have disapproved
17. 'd known
18. hadn't agreed
19. would have taken

EXERCISE 3

2. I wish the kids had brought good presents to Andy's birthday party. I wish there had been a Mrs. Potato Head toy in one of those boxes.
3. I wish Woody hadn't fought with Buzz. I wish Buzz hadn't fallen out the window.
4. I wish I hadn't lost Buzz Lightyear. I wish I'd had my favorite toy to take to Pizza Planet.
5. I wish I hadn't found out the truth about being a toy instead of a real spaceman. I wish I had been able to save the universe from evil.
6. We wish we had realized the importance of friendship. We wish we had helped each other sooner.

EXERCISE 4

2. If he hadn't sold candy to train passengers as a boy, he might not have loved model trains as an adult.
3. He would have joined the army in World War I if he hadn't been too young.
4. Disney couldn't have met his fiancée's parents if his friend Ub hadn't given him money to buy a suit.
5. If Disney hadn't needed the help of his brother Roy, he wouldn't have asked Roy to be his business partner.
6. If his art lessons hadn't meant a lot to Disney, he wouldn't have paid for lessons for Disney Studio artists.
7. Disney couldn't have made *Snow White and the Seven Dwarfs* if a bank hadn't loaned him $1.5 million.
8. If the movie hadn't succeeded, the bank would have taken Disney's home, his studio, and the film.

9. If Disney hadn't died in 1966, he would have seen the opening of the EPCOT Center in Florida.
10. He might not have overcome his unhappy childhood if he hadn't been a genius.

EXERCISE 5

4. would . . . have saved
5. had bought
6. had made
7. would . . . have gone
8. Would . . . have traveled
9. hadn't stayed
10. No, you wouldn't have
11. had called
12. would . . . have told
13. Yes, they would have
14. had planned
15. would . . . have enjoyed
16. Yes, you would have

EXERCISE 6

I just watched *Toy Story 3* on DVD. I really wish
I had see the movie sooner. I knew it was the most _(seen)_
popular movie of the summer in 2010, but I had no
idea how good it really was. Honestly, if I would have _(had)_
known about the incredible animation in the film, I
would have gone to a movie theater to see it. In fact,
I would even have pay extra to see the 3D version. _(paid)_
Yes, I know what you're thinking. You told me to
see the film when it came out. I really wish I have _(had)_
listened to you.

Luckily, I was able to download and watch *Toy Story* and *Toy Story 2*. I saw those movies a long
time ago. If I hadn't watched them again, I might _(have)_
forgotten about Andy as a little boy and the
relationships between Woody, Buzz Lightyear, and
the other toys. It was interesting to see Andy as a
college student in *Toy Story 3*. And Andy's mother
played a small but important role again. The
original *Toy Story* will never have happened if she _(would)_
hadn't given Buzz Lightyear to Andy as a birthday
gift. In *Toy Story 3*, none of the important events
would have occurred if she hadn't kept asking Andy
to clean his room and if she didn't put Andy's toys in _(hadn't)_
the garbage by mistake. Does Andy's mother remind
you of anyone? We could had had a lot more free _(have)_

time as kids if Grandma ~~weren't~~ *hadn't* always forced us to pick up our toys, but she sure gave good presents!

OK, that's all for now. You're still planning to go back home to visit Grandma next month, right? I'll see you then.

EXERCISE 7

Answers will vary.

UNIT 25 (pages 149–153)

EXERCISE 1

2. they	**10.** don't
3. me	**11.** are
4. she	**12.** they
5. was	**13.** planned
6. had taken	**14.** he
7. her	**15.** told
8. him	**16.** hadn't committed
9. 'd gotten	**17.** had scored

EXERCISE 2

2. (that) it's Wednesday.

3. (that) her husband had driven her to the interview.

4. (that) their house is near the lake.

5. (that) she'd shoplifted a lipstick once as a teenager.

6. (that) she'd gone to her mother right away.

7. (that) she'd taken her to the store to return the lipstick.

8. (that) she always tells the truth.

9. (that) the test seems easy.

10. (that) she doesn't mind taking lie-detector tests.

EXERCISE 3

3. He said (OR told the interviewer) (that) he'd been a salesclerk. That's true.

4. He said (OR told the interviewer) (that) he'd received a promotion to supervisor. That's not true.

5. He said (OR told the interviewer) (that) he'd supervised five other salesclerks. That's not true.

6. He said (OR told the interviewer) (that) he'd been a reliable employee. That's true.

7. He said (OR told the interviewer) (that) he'd shown initiative. That's true.

8. He said (OR told the interviewer) (that) his employers had liked his work. That's true.

9. He said (OR told the interviewer) (that) Bates hadn't fired him. That's true.

10. He said (OR told the interviewer) (that) he'd lost his job because of staff reductions. That's true.

11. He said (OR told the interviewer) (that) he'd earned $25,000 a year. That's not true.

12. He said (OR told the interviewer) (that) he'd gotten a raise of more than $2,000. That's not true.

EXERCISE 4

November 7

I called Jason last week and told him that I ~~'ve lost~~ *'d lost* my job. Jason was such a good friend that he offered to lend me some money, but I explained that I had saved enough to be prepared in case of an emergency. I was hoping for a job at his father's company, but Jason ~~said~~ *told* me that he wasn't aware of any available positions.

November 8

Everyone says that it ~~was~~ *is* difficult to get a job these days, but Rachel says that she ~~'d~~ *'s* always believed in me. She's my biggest supporter. She keeps telling me that ~~you~~ *I* have a great chance of finding a job soon.

November 9

I went to a job placement agency this morning to meet with a recruiter. The recruiter told *me* that she ~~wants~~ *wanted* to give me a computer skills test. After I finished the test, she said that she was very pleased with ~~your~~ *my* score on the test. In fact, she said, "I know of several jobs that you're qualified for."

November 15

The recruiter has been very helpful. I had an interview this afternoon. It went well. The manager told me that I was ~~my~~ *his* last appointment of the day. Maybe that means I'll be the first person that he thinks of when he makes his final decision. I hope so!

EXERCISE 5

Answers will vary.

EXERCISE 1

2. He said (that) he'd been living there his whole life.
3. He said (that) he'd experienced many earthquakes in his years there.
4. He said (that) that quake had been the worst.
5. He said (that) he would start to repair the damage on his house that week.
6. He said (that) he had to stay optimistic.
7. He said (that) he might get government aid the following month to restore his one-hundred-year-old home.
8. He said (that) he couldn't afford earthquake insurance right then.
9. He said (that) he had looked into it before the earthquake.
10. He said (that) he should have bought some insurance then.

EXERCISE 2

2. She said (that) she'd felt a sensation of falling.
3. He said (that) they'd all been pretty well prepared for an earthquake, but not for the fire.
4. He said (that) the walls of those buildings might collapse at any time.
5. He said (that) he hadn't seen anything like it.
6. He said (that) it had felt like a giant hand reaching down and shaking him.
7. She said (that) she was scared that there was going to be another one.
8. She said (that) she was so glad she was there.
9. She said (that) although she'd been through war in her country, she'd had no idea what to do in the quake.
10. She said (that) if her house couldn't be saved, she didn't know how she'd bear it because she'd have no place to live.

EXERCISE 3

(Answers may vary slightly.)

3. That's right. She said (that) several thousand of them might occur that day.
4. That's right. She said (that) most would go unnoticed because they would occur beneath the ocean surface.
5. That's wrong. She acknowledged (that) some had started dangerous tidal waves (tsunamis).
6. That's right. She added that the tsunami had killed hundreds of thousands of people.
7. That's wrong. She stated (that) she couldn't explain in great detail because it would be too complicated.
8. That's wrong. She indicated (that) a hidden fault had caused the 1994 Los Angeles quake.
9. That's right. She noted (that) it had had several strong quakes in the past 20 years.
10. That's right. She said (that) another interviewer had just asked her that very same question the day before.
11. That's wrong. She claimed (that) scientists might be able to make more accurate predictions sometime in the future.
12. That's right. She said (that) it was a good idea for them to have an emergency plan.

EXERCISE 4

News reports about the tsunami in the Indian Ocean on December 26, 2004, said that children *had been* ~~are~~ able to save lives that day. In a recent interview, Dr. M. T. Ito explained why. She observed that the children *had* ~~have~~ remembered their geography lessons that day.

Dr. Ito pointed out that tourists on the beaches in places like Thailand were amazed when the water of the Indian Ocean receded at the start of the tsunami. As the water pulled back, they followed it so that they could see the unusual sight. Dr. Ito said that many of the tourists *were* ~~are~~ taking photos instead of evacuating the beach. However, there were others, including children, who understood the danger. Because they knew about geography, they quickly explained that a powerful wave of water *would* ~~will~~ return in about five minutes. They told their family and friends that they *had* ~~have~~ to leave the beach and go to higher ground *right then* ~~right now~~. And once they were in a safe place, they told everyone they should stay *there* ~~here~~ because one large wave did not mean that the tsunami *was* ~~is~~ over.

In the words of Dr. Ito, "You can never know too much about Earth science." So if you're a student, pay attention in geography class. If you're not, it might be a good idea to watch the National Geographic Channel on TV.

EXERCISE 5

Answers will vary.

EXERCISE 1

2. She told me not to turn right.
3. "Slow down."
4. "Don't drive so fast."
5. She asked me to turn on the radio.
6. "Can (OR Could) you please open the window?" OR "Please open the window."
7. "Please come in for coffee." OR "Come in for coffee, please." OR "Would you like to come in for coffee?"
8. She told me not to park in the bus stop.

EXERCISE 2

3. drivers not to rely on caffeinated beverages, such as coffee or cola, to stay awake.
4. drivers to share the driving responsibilities with another person if possible to avoid fatigue.
5. drivers not to wait until they're sleepy to take a break.
6. drivers to stop every couple of hours and stretch their legs by walking around.
7. drivers to listen to music or a book on tape as a remedy for sleepiness.
8. drivers not to allow daydreaming to interfere with driving.
9. drivers not to park on the side of the road if they need to stop for a short nap.

EXERCISE 3

2. told
3. to slow
4. not to
5. to pull
6. to show
7. ordered
8. to take
9. invited
10. to wait

EXERCISE 4

2. (Please) buckle your seat belt.
3. (Please) slow down.
4. (Please) don't speed.
5. (Please) pull over and stop.
6. (Please) show me your license. OR Would you (please) show me your license?
7. (Please) give me the permit.
8. (Please) take the wheel (and follow me to the police station).
9. Would you like to have dinner at my place?
10. Could (OR Can) you wait until another day?

EXERCISE 5

My neighbor Jeanette is still a terrible driver. I
advised her ~~go~~ *to* go to driving school, but her first lesson was bad, really bad. To start with, she was drinking a large cup of hot coffee when she got in the car. The driving instructor told her ~~that~~ to throw the coffee away. He ordered her ~~no~~ *not* to have any food or drink in the vehicle during a lesson. When she turned the volume on the radio way up and began singing along with her favorite rock music, he said *to* turn the radio off. Then, just as the instructor was warning her to ~~paid~~ *pay* attention, her cell phone rang and she answered it. I can only imagine how angry he was, but of course Jeanette didn't think it was a problem. She was actually surprised that the instructor told her to get out of the car.

When Jeanette told me the story, I couldn't stop laughing—until she asked me to be her driving teacher. I mean, look at what happened the last time I got in the car with her! I said that I wouldn't give her lessons, but I agreed to call the driving school for her. I asked the instructor ~~giving~~ *to give* her a second chance. He agreed, but only if Jeanette promised to do everything that he said. He said that he would monitor her progress closely and added that if Jeanette's problems persisted, he would tell her *to* leave again. I cautioned Jeanette not to cause any more problems.

Jeanette has been lucky so far. She got her learner's permit back after that horrible night at the police station, and she might still finish driving school and get her license. And if she does get a driver's license, I know one thing for sure. I'll be the one who drives if she invites me to ~~going~~ *go* out with her.

EXERCISE 6

Answers will vary.

EXERCISE 1

2. She asked (me) whether I had time yesterday.
3. She asked (me) if I could show her some photos.
4. She asked (me) what my full name was.
5. She asked (me) who had chosen my name.
6. She asked (me) when I was born.
7. She asked (me) what country my family had come from.
8. She asked (me) where I was born.
9. She asked (me) what my biggest adventure had been.
10. She asked (me) what I was most proud of.

EXERCISE 2

2. how old he had been
3. how much it had cost
4. why he hadn't asked the name of the fruit
5. why the details had seemed so important
6. how they were going to get by
7. if (OR whether) he had some time to talk to him
8. if (OR whether) he felt comfortable there
9. if (OR whether) he remembered their trip to the circus
10. what he had worn to school
11. what his mother had cooked
12. what hobbies he had had
13. what his most important decision had been
14. what new invention he likes (OR liked) best

EXERCISE 3

3. He asked her where she had grown up.
4. He didn't ask her why she had moved to San Francisco.
5. He asked her what she had studied.
6. He asked her if (OR whether) she had worked during high school.
7. He asked her if (OR whether) she had ever lived in another country.
8. He asked her if (OR whether) she speaks (OR spoke) other languages.
9. He didn't ask her why she had named her first book *I Know Why the Caged Bird Sings*.
10. He asked her why she had started writing.
11. He didn't ask her if (OR whether) she had studied writing in school.
12. He didn't asked her how she evaluates (OR evaluated) her own work.

EXERCISE 4

After I saw the movie *Invictus*, I wanted to know more about it, so I watched several interviews with the film's director, Clint Eastwood. In each case, the interviewers asked why ~~had Eastwood decided~~ Eastwood had decided to make a movie about the 1995 South African team that won the Rugby World Cup championship. They asked how much ~~you~~ he liked sports, and they tried to find out whether the 2009 movie had a connection with the 2010 World Cup soccer tournament in South Africa. Several interviewers wanted to know if ~~was Eastwood's interest in politics~~ Eastwood's interest in politics was part of his decision to make the film. They also asked how much ~~did~~ the movie cost, especially since much of it was shot in South Africa. No one had to ask ~~who was Nelson Mandela~~ who Nelson Mandela was, but many wanted to know when the former South African president had come up with the idea of using a rugby championship to handle political problems. That was exactly the kind of question I became interested in. Because I am a sports fan, I originally wanted to learn more about the South African rugby team, the Springboks, and their captain, François Pienaar. However, I soon began to ask how Mandela could go from prisoner to presidential candidate to world leader to Nobel Prize winner. This paper will report the results of my research. It will focus on the reasons that Nelson Mandela won the 1993 Nobel Peace Prize.

EXERCISE 5

Answers will vary.

UNIT 29 (pages 171–175)

EXERCISE 1

2. why you enjoy watching sports all the time.
3. how you can watch those boring travel shows.
4. what the ultimate travel destinations are.
5. when your last vacation was?
6. if (OR whether) I'm going to take a vacation anytime soon.
7. how you're going to pay for your dream vacation?
8. how much a volunteer vacation will cost.
9. if (OR whether) people really take vacations where they have to work.
10. which organization has volunteer vacations in Africa?
11. where I should go for more information?

EXERCISE 2

2. if (OR whether) I have to be over twenty-one to go on a volunteer vacation.
3. who pays for the trip?
4. what the average cost of a volunteer vacation is?
5. if (OR whether) students on a volunteer vacation should bring any extra money?
6. if (OR whether) I'll have any free time on a volunteer vacation.
7. how long the trips usually last?
8. when most students take volunteer vacations.
9. if (OR whether) most of the volunteer opportunities are in the U.S.?
10. how far in advance I have to plan a volunteer vacation.

EXERCISE 3

2. where to look for a nonstop flight and the lowest possible airfare.
3. how to rent a car.
4. what to do about rental car insurance.
5. where to go for an inexpensive language course.
6. how long to stay in Spain.
7. what kind of clothes to pack.
8. who to talk to about hotels and restaurants.

EXERCISE 4

I don't know when ~~are you~~ *you're* leaving for your trip, but I decided to write anyway. How are you? Dan and I and the kids are all fine. Busy as usual. Tonight Dan and I got a babysitter and went to the movies (we hardly ever have the chance to go out alone). We saw a romantic comedy called *The Wedding Date*. I don't know ~~is it~~ *if it's* playing near you, but I recommend it.

I was thinking about the last time we were in San Francisco together. Can you remember where we ate ~~?~~ I know the restaurant was somewhere in Chinatown, but I can't remember what it was called.

I've been wondering why I haven't heard from Wu-lan. Do you know where ~~did he move~~ *he moved*? I'd like to write to him, but I don't know how to contact him.

Well, the summer is almost here. Let us know when ~~can you~~ *you can* come for a visit. It would be great to see you again.

EXERCISE 5

Answers will vary.